NEW DIRECTIONS FOR ADULT AND CONTINUING EDUCATION

Ralph G. Brockett, *University of Tennessee, Knoxville*
EDITOR-IN-CHIEF
Alan B. Knox, *University of Wisconsin, Madison*
CONSULTING EDITOR

Revitalizing the Residential Conference Center Environment

Edward G. Simpson, Jr.
University of Georgia

Carol E. Kasworm
University of Tennessee

EDITORS

Number 46, Summer 1990

JOSSEY-BASS INC., PUBLISHERS
San Francisco • Oxford

Revitalizing the Residential Conference Center Environment.
Edward G. Simpson, Jr., Carol E. Kasworm (eds.).
New Directions for Adult and Continuing Education, no. 46.

NEW DIRECTIONS FOR ADULT AND CONTINUING EDUCATION
Ralph G. Brockett, Editor-in-Chief
Alan B. Knox, Consulting Editor

Copyright © 1990 by Jossey-Bass Inc., Publishers
and
Jossey-Bass Limited

Copyright under International, Pan American, and Universal
Copyright Conventions. All rights reserved. No part of this issue
may be reproduced in any form—except for a brief quotation
(not to exceed 500 words) in a review or professional work—
without permission in writing from the publishers.

Microfilm copies of issues and articles are available in 16mm
and 35mm, as well as microfiche in 105mm, through University
Microfilms Inc., 300 North Zeeb Road, Ann Arbor, Michigan 48106.

NEW DIRECTIONS FOR ADULT AND CONTINUING EDUCATION is part of
The Jossey-Bass Higher Education Series and is published quarterly
by Jossey-Bass Inc., Publishers (publication number USPS 493-930).
Second-class postage paid at San Francisco, California, and at additional
mailing offices. Postmaster: Send address changes to Jossey-Bass Inc.,
Publishers, 350 Sansome Street, San Francisco, California 94104.

EDITORIAL CORRESPONDENCE should be sent to the Editor-in-Chief,
Ralph G. Brockett, Dept. of Technological and Adult Education,
University of Tennessee, 402 Claxton Addition, Knoxville,
Tennessee 37996-3400.

Library of Congress Catalog Card Number LC 85-644750

International Standard Serial Number ISSN 0195-2242

International Standard Book Number ISBN 1-55542-821-5

Cover photograph by Wernher Krutein/PHOTOVAULT, copyright © 1990.

Manufactured in the United States of America. Printed on acid-free paper.

CONTENTS

EDITORS' NOTES

The modern conference center exists in many forms—forms that feature an array of architectural designs, that offer choices from a broad spectrum of amenities, and that frequently provide the latest in educational technology. The proprietors of these centers include universities, churches, corporations, and organizations of all descriptions. With literally hundreds of conference centers operating in this country and dozens more under construction or in the planning stage, what should adult educators and conference-center professionals be seeking as the optimum conference learning environment?

This volume seeks to answer that question by examining a specific type of conference facility—the adult residential center—that has served as a prototype for the many kinds of conference centers found today. The authors believe that a residential conference center can provide a unique and educationally enhanced learning experience for adults. Using the metaphor of a "learning sanctuary" to describe the optimal living and educational environment for such a center, this book begins with discussions of the concept of the learning sanctuary, of the questions facing adult residential conference-center professionals in the 1990s, and of the six basic elements that need to be combined symbiotically to create and to maintain a viable learning sanctuary (Simpson, Chapter One).

First among the six elements is the need for understanding the residential learning experience, which can only come from a knowledge of its history and traditions (Buskey, Chapter Two). Second, the overarching mission of the residential conference center should be the achievement of the adult learner's educational objective. Strategies for curriculum design need to be flexible and varied to accommodate a profusion of adult learning styles and to create an effective learning environment (Kasworm, Chapter Three).

The learning sanctuary presents the adult learner with both tangible and intangible aspects. These aspects are well illustrated in the third element of the learning sanctuary, which involves a conference center's physical and psychological environments (Pappas, Chapter Four). The fourth element deals with hospitality in the learning sanctuary and how social

The editors wish to thank the following individuals for their assistance: Mr. Thomas Bolman, International Association of Conference Centers; Mr. Mark Harris, Highlander Research and Education Center; Professor Philip Nowlen, University of Virginia; Dr. Reginald Ponder, Camp Junaluska; Mr. Tom Schappert, IBM Management Development Center; and Mr. William Zawacki, Xerox International Center for Training and Management Development.

and cultural experiences are affected by the physical sensations—sights, sounds, and even smells—of the residential conference center (Comley, Chapter Five). These elements need to be successfully integrated to create the desired atmosphere for the learning sanctuary.

Enhancing both educational and living environments is the fifth element—technology. Adopting a flexible conceptual framework for the use of technology produces a more comfortable learning style for the adult and introduces realism into the learning sanctuary (Williams, Chapter Six). Human resources, the sixth and final element, ultimately determine whether the residential conference center can be elevated to the level of the learning sanctuary. For this to occur, the conference center's staff must understand their individual roles as well as the organization's central mission in providing a comprehensive residential learning experience (Hargis, Chapter Seven). A reflection on the previous chapters with implications for the future offers the reader an opportunity to ponder the learning sanctuary of tomorrow (Kasworm and Simpson, Chapter Eight).

Finally, for the reader who wishes to learn more about adult residential education and conference centers, there is a bibliography that addresses the history, operations, and philosophy of such centers (Buskey, Chapter Nine). When completed, this volume should provide the reader with a conceptual framework as well as practical step-by-step strategies for improving the residential adult learning experience. Further, we hope that the reader will discover topics in the conference center experience that would benefit from additional writing and research.

Edward G. Simpson, Jr., is director of the Georgia Center for Continuing Education and associate professor of adult education at the University of Georgia.

Carol E. Kasworm is associate professor of adult education at the University of Tennessee, Knoxville.

*Adult learning in modern residential conference centers offers a
valuable and unique educational experience when conference center
professionals understand the philosophical basis of that experience.*

The Residential Conference Center
as a Learning Sanctuary

Edward G. Simpson, Jr.

"Residential continuing education in the United States is massive in size
and growing rapidly" (Houle, 1971, p. 29). Such was Cyril O. Houle's comment in his essay, *Residential Continuing Education*. Almost twenty years
later, as we begin the decade of the nineties, Houle's observation is still
timely and appropriate. The growth about which he spoke has taken many
forms and directions, providing today's adult learner with a variety of
options.

In considering these options, this chapter seeks to establish an understanding about the nature of what should constitute excellence in the
experience of the residential adult conference center today. The standard
of excellence in a conference center is an ideal form described as the
"learning sanctuary." The learning sanctuary concept is relevant for conference center professionals whether their facilities are integral parts of universities or exist as franchise links in corporate chains.

One objective of this chapter is to sensitize those who use, design,
and operate today's conference centers to a philosophy or an attitude that
can enhance the adult learning experience in such centers. Achieving this
sensitivity requires analytical reflection, a bit of introspection, an understanding of the historical traditions of residential adult learning, and a
desire to conceptualize conference centers of the future. The professional
staffs of nonresidential centers can benefit by considering those elements
of the learning sanctuary that can be applied and adapted to their particular circumstances.

In an attempt to define and to facilitate analysis of the learning sanctuary, this chapter offers a series of questions that address the history,

NEW DIRECTIONS FOR ADULT AND CONTINUING EDUCATION, no. 46, Summer 1990 © Jossey-Bass Inc., Publishers   3 present, and future of residential adult learning centers. If the central mission of the conference center is to provide an enhanced learning environment for the adult student, then the questions raised herein have a relevance for professionals involved in the design and implementation of residential conferencing, as well as for adult educators and the adult learners themselves.

Understanding the Sanctuary Concept

The word "sanctuary" may provoke images as diverse as a refuge for wildlife or a place of worship. In discussing sanctuary as a metaphor for the residential center, one needs to guard against slipping into sanctimoniousness. Acknowledging that caveat, the term can still be of considerable value in capturing the spirit, feeling, or attitude that should pervade a residential conference center experience. The religious connotations for the term "sanctuary" in the Western tradition are generally acknowledged, if not always understood. Scholars of Semitic religions use the term in a broad sense, as well as in a more limited one. The broader usage denotes as a sanctuary any area associated with a deity. The narrower interpretation describes an actual place of worship having an altar or trappings of a cult (Hastings, 1963). The broad interpretation of "sanctuary" is not compatible with the residential center concept. The narrow interpretation, with its "altar" and "trappings," does suggest, as a metaphor, the "religion" of adult education as practiced in the residential-conference center. However, the definition of sanctuary that engenders the strongest sense of identification with residential centers describes it as a retreat or escape from the maelstrom of daily life. This interpretation permits life within the conference center to be viewed as relatively unhurried contemplation and study of issues contributing to an individual's disquietude. There should exist within the learning sanctuary a sense of personal and professional renewal. Or, at the very least, there should be an ambience that suggests to the adult learner that the possibility for renewal exists.

As the reader will discover from Buskey's history of the residential conference center in Chapter Two, a characteristic of sanctuary of the early "centers," particularly in the Danish folk schools, was the participant's disengagement from the normal routines of life to join with others in a retreat setting. Here in often primitive physical facilities dedicated to adult learning, individuals lived for extended periods in pursuit of specific learning objectives or personal development and enlightenment. There was opportunity for reflection and thoughtful discourse on a multitude of issues or on facets of a single issue. A process of socialization occurred between the participants, which surely must have enhanced the learning experience.

Too infrequently today do adults return from retreats or conferences where the combination of program content, social interaction, and environmental ambience, along with a variety of intangibles, have united to provide them with a sense of renewal and an enhanced educational experience. Why does this feeling occur in some conference settings, yet is so lacking in others? Does the "spiritual" success of residential adult learning in today's conference centers depend totally on serendipity? Can thoughtful professionals in the conference center "business," both in higher education and in private enterprise, create an environment that promotes and heightens these positive and exceptional experiences? Is it realistic to expect that conference center staff can be trained to understand and adopt a philosophy that has as a principle tenet the intrinsic worth of the residential experience?

Challenging professionals who design and operate conference centers to reflect on what they do is vitally important to create a successful residential conference. As to why some conference experiences create those special feelings described, serendipity always plays a role, but there is also the likelihood that many complex ingredients have been skillfully combined by professional conference planners. Clearly, thoughtful professionals can develop a conference environment that improves the quality of the adult learning experience.

For the professional, to consider historical models is to understand more completely how residential conference centers have come to be what they are. To consider them critically is to develop further those elements with merit and to discard those without. Furthermore, critical reflection by the conference professional helps restore and carry forward an understanding of residential education to a new generation.

In a conference center, it is possible for the astute professional to shape and control the physical environment, curriculum, social dimension, operating philosophy, methods of selecting and training personnel, and the cultural amenities encountered by the conferees. In essence, a largely controlled sanctuary environment is possible; consequently, when the conferee enters this environment, a series of desired psychological and physical responses, both tangible and intangible, can be heightened predictably (see Pappas's and Comley's discussions in Chapters Four and Five, respectively). The individual will have left a rather troubling and stressful world for a short respite, a period of renewal in a safe harbor. The conferee will have found a learning sanctuary.

A Perspective on the Modern Conference Center

As the movement toward that milestone in human history somewhat romantically described as "the next millennium" continues, there is no shortage of problems and issues to perplex the individual and about which many debate and reflect in the attempt to find solutions and answers. Indeed, one need only contemplate a brief list of global concerns including poverty, the "greenhouse effect," hunger, nuclear arms, pollution, and drugs to have the spirit subdued and even verge on despair. Playing against this background of possible catastrophe is the counterpoint of everyday problems, those immediately pragmatic issues that fill most lives, affecting individuals personally and professionally. Should I take the time to learn Lotus 1-2-3? Is a career change the answer? Do I really have time to be a community volunteer? When and where can I receive continuing professional education for my recertification?

Whether the issue is cosmic or local, people are constantly seeking timely and effective answers. If the issue is one that can clearly be extrapolated beyond the individual to the benefit of many, there is often a compelling need to share and discuss what may be a multitude of related permutations. This communal discussion of an important issue may include initially only family or close friends and colleagues, but if the subject holds wide interest there can be a potentially vast audience. Our ancestors considered such matters through tribal counsels. Today the nomenclature has been defined so that the tribal meeting has become the "issue conference" or "training seminar." Regardless, the gathering still requires a meeting site.

Whatever adults label their "meeting" (conference, retreat, seminar, or symposium), it is arguably one of the greatest consumers of their daily lives; a meeting exhausts that precious resource, time, and often increases physical and emotional stress. Consequently, the more efficient a meeting can be made both in content and logistics, the better one endures the stress. Thus, the pragmatic dimension of "essential" meetings and education has led to an institutionalized environment for holding such assemblies. Today's meeting needs have created the ubiquitous conference center. A product of the public and the private sector, the secular and the sectarian, the university and the corporation, the conference center today numbers in the hundreds. Regrettably, the professional staffs of conference centers are, in the main, devoid of appreciation for and understanding of their historical roots. Nevertheless, conference professionals continue to strive to educate, inform, and train adults. Frequently aided by technology, they seek to expand their communal discussions and to better inform their audiences. The conference professional often aspires to satisfy articles of faith in the creed of adult education through environmental and curriculum design. Too frequently, however, they fall short of worthwhile and attainable objectives, both educationally and environmentally, by permitting the conference center to become a creation of compromise, a physical entity and an educational concept of unfulfilled potential.

Today's residential conference center is not a product of modern technology but, instead, has its heritage in European traditions of the early nineteenth century. This heritage has produced adult conference activities that currently take place in many kinds of facilities, including hotels, university residence halls, summer camp facilities, and private homes designated for such activity. To illustrate this diversity and the spectrum of clients, one need only look at the International Association of Conference Centers (IACC). Organized in 1981 to improve understanding of these facilities within the hospitality industry, IACC, because of the diversity of conference centers, has chosen to group its membership into the following six broadly defined categories:

1. *Executive.* These facilities serve primarily upper management with planning, education, and training seminars. There are twenty-four members in IACC meeting this definition.

2. *Corporate.* There are thirteen corporate IACC members. These are defined as centers designed for parent-company use, but they may also accept some external business.

3. *Resort.* IACC has eleven members in this category. The emphasis is placed primarily on recreation and social matters, with an executive audience in mind.

4. *College and University.* These sixty-six IACC conference centers are affiliated with institutions of higher learning. The meetings held in these facilities are university-oriented and reflect a wide range of amenities. They may or may not be residential. Currently, forty-two members indicate residential capability.

5. *Other Not-for-Profit.* There are twelve members in this IACC category, some of which represent a hybrid between university and executive centers. Others are independent entities.

6. *European.* The fifteen members of IACC in this category are grouped by geography, not by any of the above classifications.

Total membership in IACC is 141 conference centers (Thomas Bolman, executive director of IACC, telephone conversation, August 1989). Clearly, the evolutionary pathways (as described in Chapter Two) leading from the Danish folk high school to the modern conference center are numerous.

Shaping the Agenda for the Residential Conference Center

Since 1986, two conferences particularly have played major roles in developing the concept of the learning sanctuary. During these two events, the first at the University of Oxford in England and the second at the University of New Hampshire, professionals in the fields of adult education and residential conferencing talked about the past, present, and future of conference centers. The papers presented at these two gatherings, in conjunction with informal discussion between the participants, began to define more clearly for this writer a contemporary agenda for the residential conference center.

The Oxford and New Hampshire Conferences. In the autumn of 1986, adult educators from various universities in the United States and the

United Kingdom met at Oxford in that university's residential adult learning center, Rewley House. The occasion was an international conference comparing and contrasting adult and continuing education in the United Kingdom with that found in the United States. A special emphasis was placed on the adult residential learning center. This emphasis seemed appropriate since the rededication of a newly expanded and remodeled Rewley House conference center had served as a catalyst for holding the meeting. Participants included residential conference center directors and adult education faculty. During the conference week, participant discussions (formal and informal) debated the status and future of residential adult learning centers.

Two years after the Oxford conference in the autumn of 1988, several members of the group who had convened at Rewley House were together on yet another occasion that underscored the importance of adult residential education. This gathering marked a watershed for the New England Center for Continuing Education, which is located on the campus of the University of New Hampshire. A major expansion and remodeling of this residential conference center had just been completed. As with Rewley House, the New England Center project had been made possible through funding by the W. K. Kellogg Foundation as a reaffirmation of its commitment to the concept of residential continuing education centers. Just as at Rewley House, there were conference sessions that dealt with the history, development, and future of residential conference centers. Although participants came only from university environments, their discussions included a variety of conference center formats.

At both conferences, participants could have taken considerable inspiration from Livingstone's "ignored educational principle": "That any subject is studied with much more interest and intelligence by those who know something of its subject-matter than by those who do not: and, conversely, that it is not profitable to study theory without some practical experience of the facts to which it relates" ([1941], 1954, p. 12).

The conferees did not provide as specific and lengthy a taxonomy of modern conference centers as does IACC. Nevertheless, the discussants believed from their research and "practical experience" in conferencing that the trend at universities in the United States seemed clearly to be moving away from unified complexes that contain educational facilities and lodging accommodations operated by the institutions themselves. Food often came through the services of a caterer or the functional but unexciting cafeteria stuck in a corner of the conference facility. Even the latter was frequently supplemented or supplanted by the omnipresent vending machine. Corporate hotels had begun to provide lodging accommodations on campuses with increasing frequency either as a component of the conference center or through a shuttle service between meeting and sleeping facilities. Generally, the concept of residential adult learning on campuses appeared to have evolved toward a utilitarian approach that often disconnected the elements that had unified the traditional residential scheme. The overarching mission of colleges and universities was delivery of the educational program. Other facilities, while important, played a secondary role.

The conferees felt the private sector could be divided into two broad categories. One grouping, composed of corporate hotel chains and conference center entrepreneurs, provided a physical environment with the user responsible for the educational program. The second category, represented by corporate business entities, was the residential training center. In this instance, staff of the corporation made a conscious effort to integrate curriculum and physical environment to achieve their organization's training and educational objectives.

If residential conference centers did exist in these broadly defined categories, what difference did it make in the quality of the residential adult learning experience? For example, there existed no formal evidence that an adult learner benefited appreciably from dining on good food in pleasant surroundings as opposed to gulping down the offerings of a coin-operated machine in a crowded hallway. This was true at university centers and corporate hotels. The effect that such differences had, participants concluded, came from the same kind of effects as what each participant purported to experience during the Oxford and New England conferences. Conferees at both conferences professed a sense of exhilaration and renewal, which at Oxford they attributed to the university's mystique, history, and inherent charm. At the New England Center they felt that a "quiet" excitement came from the beauty of a New England autumn surrounding a retreat in which the spirits of all were renewed.

In reflecting on the characteristics of the European residential adult education movement as summarized by Houle (1971, pp. 13-21), the Oxford and New Hampshire experiences had indeed given participants elements of that tradition by providing a sense of community for a relatively small group. The groups' members had taken a complete break from the normal routines of life to gather in special places, prompted by a sense of mission that was educational in character and that ultimately could benefit many. Colleagues enjoyed exceptional experiences in the learning sanctuaries that Rewley House and the New England Center for Continuing Education became for them.

Questions for the Residential Conference Center Agenda. In the context of these two conferences, the following questions emerged that help further define the agenda for residential conferencing in the 1990s. What had residential adult and continuing education become? Had it moved beyond the idea that learning could benefit measurably from a conscious effort to remove adults from their everyday environments and immerse them in an environment designed to enhance the educational experience, in part through insulation from external distractions? Conferees wondered if a holistic educational experience could be provided through group inter-action as well as through individualized, self-directed learning projects. How had the residential experience changed in the United States since 1951, when the first center for continuing education funded by the W. K. Kellogg Foundation opened on the Michigan State University campus? What had been the nature of the residential conference center's evolution on college campuses since 1936, when the first such center opened at the University of Minnesota? Had significant philosophical differences emerged between the private sector and higher education in their uses of such centers? What should be the models for residential conference centers in the 1990s? Finally, was there present in some circumstances at residential centers an ethos that was worthy of attempted replication because it enhanced the total learning experience, whether that experience was in a corporate, sectarian, or campus setting?

These questions led to more specific inquiries as to what constitutes successful residential conferencing. For example, what role does current research show that architectural and interior design plays in the creation of a physical environment that not only efficiently "processes" groups of adult learners but also provides them with a psychological orientation that fosters the learning process? In the psychological dimension, what impact is felt by the adult learner when food is colorfully and artistically presented at meal times? How can the residential conference center address the cultural and artistic interests of the adult learner, as an ancillary benefit of the primary learning experience? For example, does an environment that contains various pieces of art help create a general stimulation of the senses? Can this increase the adult learner's receptivity to the subject matter that may have been the primary reason for his or her attendance at the conference center?

Generally, everyone recognizes the importance of a professional, well-trained staff. However, are there subtle nuances that can be emphasized in the staff-training process that speak to the particular needs of the adult learner, making the learner more comfortable and thereby more receptive to the educational program? What values must be inculcated so that staff (whether administrative, program faculty, or logistical support) will under-stand the effects on adult learners of service in the learning sanctuary? How might staff be trained to understand that the residential learning center is a very different psychological environment than that of a good commercial hotel? Finally, how does this collage of psychological and phys-ical considerations blend to meet the learning needs of the adult student?

By posing these questions, the conferees at Rewley House and the New England Center for Continuing Education sought to describe some-thing that seemed to exist both as a state of mind and as a physical place—an environment that affected favorably the total person; an envi-ronment that provided not only the basics of food, lodging, meeting space, and program but that manifested a unified corporate belief that the entire residential experience could be elevated to something above the commonplace. Such a place would contain the "spiritual force" gained from its heritage in the Danish folk high school (Livingstone, 1954). Consequently, the adult learner would consciously and subliminally acknowledge the difference that distinguishes the educational experience of the learning sanctuary from other adult educational experiences or conference centers as a distinct advantage in reaching an educational or training objective. As Livingstone succinctly observed, "Education is atmosphere as well as instruction" (p. 47, 1954). The phrase that describes this "atmosphere" and also conceptualizes and communicates it is "the residential conference center as learning sanctuary."

Elements of the Learning Sanctuary

Conference centers that survive as a business provide services that are, at the very least, minimally sufficient to retain clients. Why, then, do conference centers that appear relatively equal in terms of facilities and amenities become so easily distinguishable into those that possess the characteristics of a learning sanctuary and those that do not? The simplest explanation may be an intrinsic understanding on the part of the conferee. Adults in a residential center know a "sanctuary" when they see it.

Despite the importance of an intuitive understanding of sanctuary, such an understanding must spring from certain tangible foundations. To approach systematically the development of the learning sanctuary, it is useful to think of the residential conference center as comprised of the following six integrated elements operating within a context created by the questions posed in the previous section:

1. *The Historical Context.* Goethe observed that history's best feature was the enthusiasm it raised in each of us. The history of residential education, as recounted by Buskey in Chapter Two, can have that effect when one examines the successful models of European tradition and considers the possibilities a modern setting offers to amplify the experience of the learning sanctuary. Only by understanding the beneficial educational principles that originally fostered the residential experience can one begin to understand how best to replicate a learning environment that captures such benefits.

2. *Educational Program.* The reason for a residential adult learning center should be to educate. In conference centers where this is not the case, learning will not be the priority. "Education" can occur but frequently does so in spite of competing distractions. Within a center's physical environment, no matter how attractive the amenities, all involved should subscribe to the preeminence of the learning mission. Anything less means that the educational objectives will be secondary to other considerations,

and this is contrary to the purpose of the learning sanctuary. At the core of the educational program, as Kasworm discusses in Chapter Three, should be adult educators experienced in and knowledgeable of group processes and self-directed learning strategies. These individuals can work with administrators and service staff to ensure that the educational needs of the adult learner are foremost on the agenda of the conference center.

3. *Physical Environment.* Individuals have different social needs, which are affected by the physical characteristics of the facilities and space in the learning sanctuary. Some gain a synergistic boost from interaction with numbers of people at a time. Others prefer small groups and a healthy interval away from the madding crowd, or better yet, solitude. Consequently, environmental designs should take into consideration group and individual needs and preferences. While the interaction between conferees afforded by a residential center is extremely desirable, the opportunity to reflect and work alone (to have a sanctuary within the sanctuary) can be essential, particularly for residential experiences of an extended time.

The physical space that the learning sanctuary provides for these activities can increase the conferee's feeling of security. For example, interior designers can enhance and soften building spaces through the use of live and artificial plants. The pantheistic heritage, which provides the view of the sanctuary as a natural haven, may well suggest the use of plants to create a natural or softened feeling to conference facilities. As Vick has noted ". . . like soft background music and diffused lighting, plants (or the illusion of plants) provide a measure of psychological well-being in an otherwise sterile environment" (p. 30, 1989). As Pappas discusses in Chapter Four, the design of the physical facilities should take into consideration the special needs of the adult learner.

4. *The Support Services Context.* Closely related to the effects produced by the physical environment are those effects generated by the social characteristics of the learning sanctuary. Elements of the social atmosphere include "things" as well as people. Attention should be paid to textures of surfaces, to sound, to color, and to cleanliness. The learning sanctuary should provide opportunities for recreation and diversion so that conferees can also experience noncompulsory learning experiences that refresh them and prepare them to address their primary learning objectives. Such experiences cover a wide spectrum from physical exercise to fine food and entertainment, to the arts, to a garden, to a variety of amenities that belong to a learning sanctuary's geographical location. For example, consider how the history and charm of Rewley House and its placement among the colleges of Oxford University contribute to the sense of sanctuary the House provides. There should exist within the learning sanctuary's environment a sense of refinement. For example, while nourishment is a necessity, should our partaking of it always occur within the plastic world of a fast-food enterprise? As Comley explains in Chapter Five, while expediency

and speed have their places so, too, does refined dining offered by a well-trained staff.

5. *Technology.* A learning sanctuary without technology is unacceptable. Just as the modern agriculturist would not consider forsaking science and technology for a return to cultivation with a sharpened stick and a rain dance, neither can the adult learner be deprived of a technology-enhanced educational environment. Today, the difficulty with learning technology in the residential center is often not its absence but its cloying, suffocating presence. Adults reared on the lecture and the blackboard can be intimidated by terms like "computer-assisted instruction," "hyper media," "interactive video," "uplink," and "asynchronous telecommunication." To achieve the psychological and environmental conditions desired, the technology component should be provided in a nonthreatening and helping manner. Further, the educational program should be designed so that technology can be incorporated in a fashion that enhances the effectiveness of the curriculum. The educational program should never be distorted for the primary purpose of incorporating technology. Actually, the technology should be "invisible" to the adult learner and its usage should contribute to the learner's sense of well-being within the learning sanctuary. Williams discusses concepts of technology-enhanced learning in Chapter Six.

6. *Human Resources.* The learning sanctuary can be realized only if its most crucial element is successful—the people who administer, program, and operate it. As Hargis notes in Chapter Seven, each staff member must understand the mission and the importance each has in fulfilling it. This requires careful selection, orientation, training, and ongoing human-resource development. A maid in lodging services or a carpenter in the physical-plant department may understandably have difficulty seeing his or her mission as an educational quest to help the adult learner; yet the learning sanctuary that is unclean or in disrepair fails to create the special sense of place it needs to be effective. Just as importantly, the educational-programming specialist must not view his or her role as inherently superior to that of others. True, the educational experience should be the preeminent objective, but people in a variety of capacities within the residential conference center must share in the vision and sense of mission of the center if its purpose as a learning sanctuary is to be achieved. Those individuals with roles of administrative leadership have the responsibilities of articulating that vision and of never ceasing to work for its inculcation in the values of all personnel.

Faith in the Residential Conference Experience

While there may be a number of motivations for building a residential conference center, ranging from simply making money to improving learning, the primary issue for an adult educator should be educational effectiveness (Kafka and Griffith, 1984). As Kafka and Griffith observed, ". . . the decision to build a residential center has been based more on faith in its educational effectiveness than on empirical demonstrations of the superiority of this method of adult education" (1984, p. 19). In fact, their study led them to conclude ". . . that personal and program differences have more to do with differences in the amount of learning taking place at residential centers than does the mere fact of residence" (p. 25).

Does this finding render moot consideration of the residential conference center as a learning sanctuary? Certainly, it does not! Indeed, one of the conference groups studied by Kafka and Griffith clearly benefited from the residential experience because of the socialization that took place there (p. 25). The learning sanctuary has extant within it an element of serendipity that can at any time bring forth an enhancement of the learning experience by the very fact of its being a residence. Such possibilities caused by chance grow more likely if thoughtful preparation is made beforehand.

In summary, the experience described in this chapter of what should constitute the learning sanctuary is in reality a case for the education of the whole person. If we are aware of the residential tradition and sensitive to the adult learner's psychological well-being, then whatever the design of our conference centers, the "education" should be improved.

References

Hastings, J., Grant, F. C., and Rowley, H. H. (eds.). *Dictionary of the Bible.* (Rev. ed.) New York: Scribner's, 1963.

Houle, C. O. *Residential Continuing Education.* Notes and Essays on Education for Adults, no. 70. Syracuse, N.Y.: Syracuse University Publications in Continuing Education, 1971.

Livingstone, R. W. "The Future in Education." In *On Education.* Cambridge, England: Cambridge University Press, 1954. (Originally published 1941.)

Kafka, J. J., and Griffith, W. S. "Assessing the Effectiveness of Residential Adult Education." *Continuum,* 1984, *48* (1), 19–26.

Vick, R. "Artificial Nature: The Synthetic Landscape of the Future." *The Futurist,* 1989, *23* (4), 29–32.

Edward G. Simpson, Jr., is director of the Georgia Center for Continuing Education and associate professor of adult education at the University of Georgia. He consults and writes on issues related to continuing education centers.

To understand the contemporary residential center one must examine its history and traditions.

Historical Context and Contemporary Setting of the Learning Sanctuary

John H. Buskey

Residential adult education has its roots in three concepts: adult students, who are the participants involved in the learning activities; residence, which means that the participants live and eat together in a common facility; and education, which is the spiritual aim of the experience. Initially, residential adult education meant just that—adults living and studying together in a common facility, in many ways learning within a sanctuary like setting. Over the years, the concepts about and the facilities in which this kind of learning takes place have undergone a metamorphosis such that a much wider array of facilities, programming, and learners has become available than was initially imagined. Today, one rarely hears the term residential adult education; instead, people talk about conference centers, which tends to focus discussion primarily on facilities, implying perhaps a wider range of purposes and activities, illustrated by the tremendous diversity of shapes, sizes, colors, and purposes that characterize both public and private, commercial and institutional facilities.

A Brief History of Residential Adult Education in Europe

In order to appreciate contemporary issues and trends in residential adult education, it is important to understand the historical roots of the movement that began it, the values or advantages attributed to residential programs, and the development of programs and facilities over the past century and a half. Most of the early residential adult education centers

NEW DIRECTIONS FOR ADULT AND CONTINUING EDUCATION, no. 46, Summer 1990 ©Jossey-Bass Inc., Publishers were modest, even primitive, residential facilities. All were buildings constructed for other purposes and converted to educational purposes. The facilities included crude sleeping accommodations; meeting, classroom, or learning spaces; and dining facilities. The idea of residential continuing education can be traced directly to the ideas of Bishop N.S.F. Grundtvig, a Danish philosopher and theologian of the early nineteenth century. Inspired by a prolonged study visit from 1829 to 1831 to Great Britain's Oxford and Cambridge residential universities, Grundtvig proposed the establishment of a "school for life, not for living," as a vehicle to restore Denmark's national pride and economic vitality (Grundtvig and Alford, 1965).

Grundtvig's ideas led Christen Kold to establish the first folk high school in 1851 at Ryslinge, Denmark. Young adult Danes came to Kold's folk high school to live in residence for several months at a time during the long Danish winters. There, through lectures and discussions with resident tutors, they studied social issues, government, national political and economic movements, philosophy, theology, and other cultural issues. In a careful and enlightening analysis of Grundtvig's contribution to the concept of andragogy, Warren notes that students were "encouraged to bloom rather than be educated to conform. The educational operative of encouragement, the living word [oral interaction], would foster three important interplays: teacher-student, student-student, national poet-educational community" (1989, p. 216). These three interplays formed the operational base of the folk high school, which Grundtvig postulated. The folk high school had eight distinct features:

> (a) Subject matter would not be significant; most important would be if both teacher and students are interested in whatever they choose for study; (b) dialogue should be the tool of instructional communication; (c) no tests, grades, or degrees would be imposed on students; (d) duration of a student's stay would be limited: usually one term of three or four months; on rare occasions, two consecutive terms; (e) students must live at the school during the term; (f) students would work together on some form of physical enterprise; (g) each term's educational community would be self-governing; and (h) teachers would live at the folk high school along with the students [Warren, 1989, 217-218].

The folk high schools were established during very difficult and trying times in Denmark and the impetus provided by the schools encouraged the development of progressive land, economic, and political reforms.

The curriculum, or subject matter, of the Danish and other European folk high schools ranged widely. Kold's school, for example, was non-vocational and focused on religion through study of the Bible and on nationalism by studying the Danish language, legends, and literature. With essentially a humanistic focus, its goal was the development of a spirit of inquiry (Alford, 1966). Other schools developed vocational programs, while some focused on physical fitness, the cooperative movement, liberal education, the Christian ethic, socialism, and other topics.

Each Danish folk high school was an independent institution, usually privately owned and operated by its principal, or *Vorstander* (Alford, 1966). "The . . . Vorstander does in fact stand in front, as his title implies, and is not merely first among equals. In the more traditional schools, people remain standing until he is seated, he is served first at meals, and, in countless direct or subtle ways, he makes it clear that he is the symbolic embodiment of the entire institution" (Houle, 1971, pp. 15-16).

Over the years, the forms and ideals of the folk high schools were exported to many other countries in Europe and on other continents. The movement spread rapidly throughout the rural areas in Scandinavian countries in the 1800s (Jessup, 1972, pp. 5-13) and during the quarter century between World Wars I and II, schools were established in most European countries and in Japan and India. Most were modeled on the Danish folk high school pattern, although subject matter, methods, and style varied from school to school. Some schools concentrated on vocational skills, others on physical fitness, and others studied specific religious ideas. In the 1930s, for example, Sir Richard Livingstone, an eminent British classical scholar at Oxford, visited Denmark and brought the folk-high-school idea back to Great Britain. Livingstone proposed that residential adult education be a major vehicle in the reconstruction of post-World War II Britain (Livingstone, 1954), and the increased number of British residential schools for adults in the post-war period was an outgrowth of his proposal.

Students of European residential adult education have tried to identify the unique attributes or characteristics of the movement, particularly as such students sought to transplant the ideas from one culture to another. As interpreted and summarized by Houle (1971, pp. 13-21), ten essential characteristics of the European folk high school conception have been identified:

1. *"Residential adult education requires its own physical facilities, preferably* [facilities] *which are devoted solely to the purposes"* of learning in residence.
2. *"European centers have myriad forms of sponsorship,"* ranging from independent centers, to churches, to those operated by government agencies. (It is interesting to note that few, if any, of the earlier centers were operated by universities.)
3. *"Each center has a strong central purpose which pervades the institution and which it promotes with a sense of mission."*
4. *"Whatever the specific sense of mission, it has a strongly humanistic quality.* Learning is its own reward"; resident teaching and administrative staff are "chosen in terms of the central mission of the institution."

5. *"The center has a separate identity of its own."* It is often set apart geographically or symbolically, perhaps in beautiful natural surroundings—often times in a retreat setting.

6. *"Each conference is composed of a small enough group so that everyone may establish his own identity within it."*

7. *"The center fosters a sense of community which leads the individual to enlarge his knowledge of others and of himself in relation to others."*

8. *"The conference [experience] provides a complete break from the normal processes of life of those who come to it."* Participants are detached from the normal routines of work, family and social life.

9. *"The purpose of the center is wholly educational."*

10. *"The participants in residential adult education are expected to become better citizens of their nation and of the world."*

The development of European folk high schools with these characteristics provided a substantial and rich base of philosophical ideas, program concepts, and administrative experience for the experimental efforts of those interested in transplanting the movement to North America.

Transplanting the European Tradition to North America

Attempts to transfer the residential adult education concept from Europe to North America have met with mixed success. Scandinavians who came to the upper midwest tried to recreate the folk high school here, including such schools as Danebod in Minnesota and Elk Horn in Iowa. Although the schools were successful during the first wave of Scandinavian immigrants, "the acculturation process experienced by the second generation undermined their viability," and none of them were successful over an extended period of time (Kulich, 1984, p. 11). Other schools based on the Danish model, such as the John C. Campbell Folk School, with its focus on crafts, and the Highlander Research and Education Center, whose purpose is to promote human justice and dignity (Draves, 1985, p. 82), were successfully established in the Appalachian mountains of North Carolina and Tennessee, respectively. Many of the early residential adult education centers in the United States and Canada focused their programming on specific themes, such as religion, crafts, public affairs, liberal education, and so forth. The continued success of the Campbell school and the Highlander Center seems to result from a combination of their leadership and their focus on a specific mission.

While the European folk school traditions have contributed to the development of residential adult education in America, there have been many other parallel and similar ventures initiated here with uniquely American qualities. Houle (1971, pp. 23–24) identified four of the most important early, or seminal, efforts.

The Religiously Oriented Camp Meeting or Retreat. Perhaps the most famous of these ventures is Chautauqua Institution, founded in 1874, and still operating today on the shores of Lake Chautauqua in upstate New York as a summer-long center for religious, literary, and artistic study. It was the model for the programs and facilities of numerous other organizations throughout the United States. Many religious organizations have constructed or remodeled facilities for ongoing retreats and conferences for youth and adults.

The Agricultural Short Course. Grattan (1955, pp. 200–203) reports that throughout the 1800s various local and state agricultural societies, and organizations such as the Grange, focused their energies on helping farmers improve their agricultural practices through fairs and meetings. Two- to five-day farmers' institutes were initiated in Massachusetts in 1863. Later, in the 1890s and early 1900s, the land-grant colleges began to undertake some limited instructional efforts for farmers through the establishment of early forms of the agricultural extension service. Thus, a tradition began among agriculturists to attend short courses, often on college campuses, to learn specific ways to improve farming and husbandry practices.

The University Summer Session. In the late 1800s, colleges in North America began to offer a variety of summer workshops and institutes, primarily to school teachers, in an effort to provide in-service education for an expanding teacher population that had little formal training. Over the years the university summer session has developed in many directions but continues to offer a wide range of short summer conferences, institutes, and workshops to teachers and other adult populations.

Conventions and Conferences. A more recent phenomenon, national as well as international, has been the explosive growth of meetings, conventions, and conferences for all sectors of the population. Such events are convened for a wide variety of purposes—political, educational, economic, organizational, and governmental, to name a few. They take place in all kinds of facilities, from specially designed conference facilities, to office buildings, and hotels; they are hosted by institutions of higher education, by associations, by government agencies, by businesses, and by voluntary organizations.

From the European and North American traditions of adult residential education programs, and the characteristics of the small, relatively crude facilities that housed many of these programs, concepts and ideas slowly emerged that led to the development of special modern facilities in which such programs could best be conducted. As colleges and universities began to conduct more and more conferences, workshops, and other short-term learning programs, the coordination and operation of such events gradually moved from the responsibility of an individual faculty member to a specially created conferences-and-institutes office. The next logical step was the design of more adequate physical facilities that would provide services and space necessary for the effective conduct of programs.

The Development of Modern Conference Centers

The first university-sponsored American center designed and constructed expressly for residential adult education was opened in 1936 at the University of Minnesota, financed partially by the Works Progress Administration (*Directory*, 1968). The Minnesota center incorporated sleeping rooms, dining facilities, meeting rooms, and staff offices under one roof. Program participants could live and study in isolation from their normal daily routines, with all of their normal living and learning needs effectively accommodated in one facility. The new center did not escape the scrutiny of continuing education administrators at other universities, and shortly after World War II a number of institutions pioneered the concept in different ways. Syracuse University received Pinebrook as a gift in 1948, remodeled it, and operated it for many years during the summer as a retreat center (*Directory*, 1968). The University of Illinois similarly converted Allerton House, an elegant mansion with elaborate formal gardens given to the university in 1949 and used to this day for conferences (*Directory*, 1968).

Arguably, the most significant event in post–World War II North American residential adult education took place in 1951 with the opening of the W. K. Kellogg Center for Continuing Education at Michigan State University (Houle, 1971). Essentially a collaborative effort of the W. K. Kellogg Foundation and the university, the Kellogg Center attracted enormous national and international attention and was probably the single most important event in forecasting the future of residential adult education in the United States.

As part of their contributions to the construction of continuing education centers, the W. K. Kellogg Foundation often made program grants that focused either on programming in the centers, or on the formal, graduate level preparation of adult and continuing educators. One of these grants, for example, was to the University of Chicago's Department of Education for a "Studies and Training Program in Continuing Education," under the leadership of Cyril O. Houle. The program, which was in operation for over a decade during the 1960s, provided one-year internships for graduate study in the department and a parallel practical internship in the center. A second component of the program was the conduct and support of a variety of research studies, which are reported in Houle's integrative summary of residential continuing education (1971). The program published a series of occasional "Continuing Education Reports," which described various research projects and provided a point of national focus on residential continuing education throughout the 1960s.

Just twelve blocks away from the University of Chicago campus was another organization that had an interest in residential adult education. The Center for the Study of Liberal Education for Adults was established in the early 1950s with a grant from the Fund for Adult Education to work with universities providing liberal education for adults. The CSLEA, as it was popularly known, published over 100 monographs and papers, several of which directly or indirectly addressed issues and problems in residential adult education (some are cited in this chapter). In addition, members of the staff collaborated actively with the Conferences and Institutes Division of the National University Extension Association in conducting conferences and seminars and preparing reports that dealt were developing more effective residential learning experiences for adults attending the wide variety of conferences and seminars sponsored by the member schools.

The efforts of these two programs, which often collaborated with each other, provided a rich leavening experience from the middle 1950s to about 1970. They reinforced each other, provided visibility for and nurturing of the concept of residential adult education, and enhanced both programming and the development of facilities. Unfortunately, both programs concluded their active involvement in residential adult education around 1970, and the lessons learned by a generation of people concerned with programming in the residential learning environment slowly faded until today there are only a few involved in conference-center work who are fully aware of the basic tenets of residential continuing education.

Over the intervening years, the Kellogg Foundation received dozens of formal proposals for the programming and construction of conference centers. The foundation has supported construction or remodeling of twelve continuing education centers at public and private institutions, one at the University of Oxford in England and the rest in the United States. Each had a program or physical characteristic that was unique to it; most are (or were) residential. Ten of the group are still operating. But this is just the tip of the iceberg! Many institutions that did not receive funding from the Kellogg Foundation turned their ideas and plans into proposals to other foundations, to their own universities, to state legislatures and government agencies, to private donors, to associations, to private developers, to alumni, and to university development offices for capital campaigns. There are probably well over 200 conference centers at institutions of higher education in this country alone, and more are being constructed every year.

Roughly paralleling the increased development and construction of university conference centers from the 1960s to the present day has been a similar substantial increase in the number of private commercial and non-profit conference centers. The private centers are owned and operated by many kinds of organizations, including large, multinational corporations such as IBM, Xerox, and Merrill Lynch; by conference center management companies such as Harrison Conference Services and the Marriott Corporation; by independent corporations such as the Tarrytown House Executive Conference Center, Tarrytown, N.Y., and the Arrowwood Center, Ryebrook, N.Y.; and by nonprofit organizations such as YMCAs, churches, and foundations. Facilities are located in such diverse places as resorts, rural areas, small towns, suburbia, and urban downtown office buildings. Most are residential, but increasing numbers are nonresidential centers in downtown office buildings. Until about ten to fifteen years ago, there was very little interaction between the university centers and the private centers; however, since the 1981 founding of the International Association of Conference Centers (IACC), there has been a noticeable increase in communication, a number of joint ventures, and the development of a mutual respect between center staffs for the talents and concerns of each other. The association's membership increased fifty percent in 1987 and now totals over 140 active members, including more than a dozen centers in other countries. Continued growth in the near future seems assured. According to the executive director of IACC, Thomas Bolman, there is renewed interest in the United Kingdom and Scandinavia in developing both new facilities and ongoing relationships with American conference-center professionals, and for the first time, there are initial efforts underway in Japan to develop centers there (telephone interview, November 1989).

Some Advantages of Residential Adult Education

Inherent in the practice and philosophy of residential adult education is a key set of values. Many believe that the success of residential adult education emerges from six fundamental virtues or advantages as described by Schacht (1960, pp. 2-4):

1. The advantage of *detachment,* as when one withdraws physically and psychologically from normal daily activities to study and reflect.

2. The advantage of a *change in environment* to a new and different place where he or she can feel free to experiment with new ideas in a supportive setting.

3. The advantage of *concentration* where learning can be a primary activity, with education scheduled at all hours, and where the whole person can become involved in the learning process without gaps for work and family responsibilities.

4. The advantage of *time* for the learning process which allows for absorption, assimilation, integration, practice and application.

5. The advantage of *intimacy* wherein constant association at meals, in sessions, in outdoor activities, or in the living room, encourages the process of becoming acquainted with others, which in turn facilitates the formal learning.

6. The advantage of *community,* wherein people live together in a group larger than the normal family. Members of the group from different disciplines,

backgrounds, jobs, and family situations, with different dispositions and interests provide feedback and growth experiences facilitative of further formal and informal learning.

These "advantages" have been written about widely in the literature and are clearly inherent in Houle's list of essential characteristics of European centers. They seem to permeate the general expectation of what a "residential experience" should be.

Residential Centers in Contemporary Society: The New Versus the Old

Early residential centers were small, self-contained, usually rural facilities combining residence and learning facilities in one building. They focused on a single program and participant group at a time, employed their own resident teaching staff, and focused on a single theme or subject matter, which they taught in subsequent sessions to new groups of participants. The early folk high schools provided a retreat from daily life into an extended sanctuary like learning setting where the school's educational program was anchored in a strong humanistic and theological base. They were committed to teaching values and philosophy under the tutelage of a strong and demanding tutor. The programs were several weeks or months in length, and the overriding emphasis was on the school and its purpose. The development of the whole person was the major focus of the folk high schools.

In contrast, today's typical modern conference center is a much larger facility, and it may or may not include all living and learning components in one building. Normally it employs individual specialists to design and conduct an individual program, and seldom are these specialists regular employees of the center; more often they are university faculty, government specialists, or business people with special expertise. They do not reside at the center; when they have finished their part in the program, they go their separate ways. The resident staff are administrators who specialize in coordinating the planning process to develop effective programs for adults, but who are not specialists in the subject matter of the programs, as was the *Vorstander* and his tutors. The center houses multiple programs simultaneously, and the overriding emphasis is on individual programs representing a multitude of purposes in a multitude of disciplines. In the modern center, the goals are inherent in the conferences, seminars, and workshops, not in the center, as in the original tradition. The resident staff of today's multipurpose centers focus on instructional and planning processes and techniques, rather than on subject matter based on the center's organizational mission or purpose. A further focus is on the individual as a student of a particular topic, seldom on the development of the whole person.

As we think about the modern conference center and how it is used or can be used, we tend to think of it primarily, if not solely, as a place to educate people—to conduct conferences, seminars, workshops, and other events for groups of people. In addition to such uses, Houle (1965, pp. 1–2) has proposed that the center can make two additional contributions to the university. First, the center is a potential means of educating the future leaders of the adult educational movement, a particularly viable opportunity if links are made between centers and graduate programs in adult education at universities. Second, centers may serve as a place for the conduct of research into a wide array of academic disciplines, especially those disciplines interested in human behavior as it relates to learning in adulthood. The use of centers for training and research purposes encourages a closer tie with the host (or other) university and the profession and creates the opportunity for the center to examine some of the assumptions on which its programming is based; this is a useful notion, considering the contrast between the original conception of residential adult education and today's practice.

Conclusion

While adult educators and their partners have constructed elaborate, often elegant, continuing education facilities to achieve the goal of lifelong learning, such facilities, because of their size, design, and staffing patterns, often make it difficult to conduct the kind of learning experience that truly achieves the desired goal. Many newer staff members in conference centers may not be aware of the historical and philosophical roots of residential adult education, and therefore may not be aware of some of the contributions that such concepts and traditions could make to present-day programming. There are many opportunities to enhance programming, for which the ideas of the early pioneers can be a rich source of inspiration.

References

Alford, H. G. "A History of Residential Adult Education." Abstract, unpublished Ph.D. dissertation, Department of Education, University of Chicago, June 1966.

A Directory of Residential Continuing Education Centers in the United States, Canada and Abroad, 1967–68. Chicago: Studies and Training in Continuing Education, University of Chicago, 1968.

Draves, W. A. "Analyzing Trends in Conference Design." In P. J. Ilsley (ed.), Improving Conference Design and Outcomes. New Directions for Continuing Education, no. 28. San Francisco: Jossey-Bass, 1985.

Grattan, C. H. In Quest of Knowledge. New York: Association Press, 1955.

Grundtvig, N.S.F., and Alford, H. J. "The School for Life." Continuing Education Report No. 5. Chicago: University of Chicago, 1965.

Houle, C. O. "University-Level Continuing Education." Continuing Education Report No. 7. Chicago: University of Chicago, 1965.

Houle, C. O. *Residential Continuing Education*. Notes and Essays on Education for Adults, no. 70. Syracuse, N.Y.: Syracuse University Publications in Continuing Education, 1971.

Jessup, F. W. *Historical and Cultural Influences upon the Development of Residential Centers for Continuing Education*. Occasional Papers, no. 31. Syracuse, N.Y.: Syracuse University Publications in Continuing Education, 1972.

Kulich, J. "N.S.F. Grundtvig's Folk High School Idea and the Challenges of Our Times." *Lifelong Learning*, 1984, 7 (4), 10–13.

Livingstone, R. W. "The Future in Education." In *On Education*. Cambridge, England: Cambridge University Press, 1954. (Originally published 1941.)

Schacht, R. H. *Week-End Learning in the United States*. Notes and Essays on Education for Adults, no. 29. Chicago: Center for the Study of Liberal Education for Adults, 1960.

Warren, C. "Andragogy and N.S.F. Grundtvig: A Critical Link." *Adult Education Quarterly*, 1989, 39 (4), 211–223.

John H. Buskey is associate provost for conferences and continuing education and associate professor of educational leadership at Miami University, Oxford, Ohio. He is an author, consultant, and speaker on the design, programming, and administration of conference facilities.

The learning sanctuary must provide more than effective classroom instruction.

The Learning Sanctuary as an Educational Environment

Carol E. Kasworm

What is the significance of a residential adult learning experience? Gardner (1964) suggests that a break in the patterns of our lives reveals to us our past imprisoned perspectives, perspectives that have been protected "by the comfortable web we have woven around ourselves . . ." (p. 9). Clearly this changing of perspectives is at the heart of effective residential learning. The residential education experience purposely separates adult learners from their daily routines, creating an "island" to distance mind and body from daily realities. This separation is believed to be an important leavening ingredient in the environment that helps promote change in the learner. By providing such a separation, a dedicated educational facility with a residential environment is seen by some professionals as particularly supportive of effective adult learning. However, residential education is more than the outward structures of a conference center, dining and sleeping facilities, and classrooms with instructional supports. The residential learning experience suggests an environment of ideas and actions supporting full adult learning and reflection. This chapter will explore various elements that enhance and optimize adult residential education in a learning sanctuary.

A learning sanctuary is a carefully designed living and learning residential environment. This sanctuary focuses on each participant who will experience an environment of other adult learners, as well as facilities, educators, support services, and personnel specializing in adult learning. The setting is designed to maximize these learning interactions, with both an internal architecture and an educational immersion program enhancing the learner's involvement. As suggested by Bruner (1973), effective learning experiences go beyond the information given. The learning sanctuary assumes that adults frame private meanings from these public encounters with the instructional experience, the learning group, and the residential facilities.

Each learning sanctuary is, in a real sense, an image of possibilities and ideals, and each educational environment will be unique in its embodiment of the ideals of a learning sanctuary. However, the unique perspectives of a learning sanctuary challenge the traditional concepts of program planning for adults. These perspectives highlight the importance of having adult educators who view learning through the adult participant's eyes. Unlike a short-term classroom instructional experience, the residential experience presents the paradox and possibilities of an adult in a public and private journey of learning. Part of this journey looks to the educational program and the living-learning environment to facilitate the formal instructional agenda; of equal importance, other segments of the program and the environment must carefully support and nourish the informal and self-directed learning of the adult participants.

The residential environment should not become a "place set apart" from the world of application and action. Although the learning sanctuary is on purpose designed to be separated from the daily world, the paradox of adult learning acknowledges the importance to adults of action in the real world. A key focus of the learning sanctuary is enhancement of the adult student's knowledge base, personal behavior, and intentions for action in the adult world beyond the learning sanctuary.

Perspectives on Learners' Involvement

Traditional residential educators assume that, during residence, the key adult learner experiences occur within the classroom. Thus, most program planning focuses on in-class instruction, with some concern for events outside of class, such as social gatherings. However, the framework of a learning sanctuary challenges this idea.

Instructional Focus. How should we characterize the instructional program design in a learning sanctuary? Although a residential educational program has classroom instructional activities as its core, these events represent, at best, 35 percent of learner involvement in the residential setting. The time dedicated to classroom instruction is important, because it provides the key information of the educational program. Such instruction focuses the student on key meanings and the communication of key knowledge, facts, and perspectives.

However, there are serious limitations to classroom instruction, as defined one-way communications from an instructor. From my observations, the typical adult learner maintains adequate attention to traditional lectures for approximately thirty to sixty minutes in one seating. At this point, the learner often reaches "sensory overload" and experiences fatigue or difficulty in adequately processing information. Of more serious concern, a few studies have found that information communicated solely within traditional lectures is often the least likely to be retained. For example, one study suggested that learners retained only 20 percent of key messages in a lecture. This same study noted that the retention level is enhanced by using multiple communication and participation tools (sight, hearing, reading, images, and learner's direct action and meaningful application of information) ("How Do We Learn?", n.d.). Thus, a day-long program (six to eight hours of learner involvement), should reflect diverse instructional strategies, adequate rest breaks, and specific learner-active involvement and application of information.

The residential learning experience provides an ideal environment to enhance effective adult learning. In a residential context, the planner and instructors can use the traditional classroom lecture as one form of learning, but also design a more complex and stimulating experience. The residential context supports the use of varied learning settings other than the traditional one-way approach: participatory instructional activities with learners in active dialogue and applications; involvement with various educational tools, such as computers, audio-visual devices, library resources, and off-site tours; and group and individual learning assignments, case-study analyses, or simulations.

Out-of-Class Focus. Aside from formal instructional time, the learner has approximately 35 percent of a given day for personal agendas, social interaction, relaxation, and physical support (for example, eating, exercising), and 30 percent in solitary rest and sleep. The program planner should be as concerned for this 65 percent of the learner's time as with the 35 percent spent in the classroom. The learning sanctuary should be committed to these hours as important learning time. However, this time should not be "programmed" for lock-step involvement. The program planner should construct environmentally supported options for diverse adult learner personal agendas. On occasion, certain learner groups and specialty programs commit their adult learners to a comprehensive educational experience with a fourteen- to sixteen-hour program structure. These types of programs reflect organizer's beliefs in group development, with key continuous involvements in informal, yet orchestrated, learning settings.

How should a program planner approach these out-of-class experiences? Adult learners are more effective learners when their human needs are addressed. Each residential experience should incorporate strategies for development by the individual learner of a supportive identity in the learning group, the opportunity to develop collegial friendships, the necessary time and resources to pursue personal learning agendas, and the acknowledgment that each learner must both act and reflect on his or her public and private learning journey (Knowles, 1980). For example, the program planner includes breaks, meals, and social hours for small group gatherings. Yet the planner needs to recognize that adults will want to engage in these interactions according to their own personal style and sense of identity. Evening events should be sufficiently diverse to support the learners' cultural backgrounds, as well as to enhance the broad mission of the educational program. Further, these evening events are often opportunities for playful moments of relaxation and divergent thinking. As noted by psychologists who have studied creative problem-solving, the changing of mood, place, and context can facilitate significant insights. These interactions develop a set of communal values and group meanings for the learning experiences (Collins, 1985). These group meanings are as important to the learner as the potential understandings and perspectives developed within the classroom context.

Planning Context. The above discussion considered "in-class" and "out-of-class" learner time as a planning framework for learner involvement often used by program designers. This framework can be helpful in guiding program planners in their design of a learner's experience in a residential setting. However, designing a residential learning experience using this framework alone is often simplistic and superficial. A learning sanctuary reflects a total learning environment interacting with the adult learner. Thus, the program planner must look beyond the dimension of committed learner time to specific instructional actions and involvements. This chapter will suggest that educational planners and designers should consider the multidimensionality of the environment and learning experiences. Effective residential learning is based on a holistic and environmentally based perspective, a Master Plan for the Learning Sanctuary.

Master Plan for a Learning Environment

The Master Plan for the Learning Sanctuary, grounded in a philosophy and a value perspective of adult learning, features four core elements that guide both the design and implementation of the learning sanctuary. This master plan includes four core elements: (1) the specific design of a learning culture, (2) the dynamics of experiential learner participation, (3) the holistic involvement of the learner in the environment, and (4) the learning sanctuary's commitment to fostering self-directed learning. These elements, as well as the more traditional planning frameworks of time logistics and learner involvement provide the learner, the educational planner, the instructional staff, and the support personnel with common goals, common beliefs, and expected common outcomes.

The Sanctuary as a Learning Culture. At the heart of an effective residential educational program or center is a purposely designed, continuously nourished learning culture. This learning culture reflects the belief in adult educators as "master architects" of a total learning and living environment. Further it reflects the key values of the specific learning sanctuary through the images, values, and actions of both the instructional events and the psychological and physical supporting environment. Each learning culture has a clearly identified mission committed to the education of the adult learner within a living-learning environment. It offers a vision to guide instructional and logistical staff as they create temporary learning communities.

For example, the Highlander Center at New Market, Tennessee, a residential center committed to social change, states in its 1987 mission statement that it "seeks to create educational experiences that empower people to take democratic leadership towards fundamental change." This center has a lengthy history of involvement with social issues, labor unions, civil rights, and environmental concerns. With its emphasis on empowerment, this center is focused on creating a "dynamic process of ownership" where individual participants are expected to give input in shaping the learning processes. The educational staff stipulates a preference for a minimum of two people from a community to attend and participate in their workshops. These two or more individuals are expected to become co-supporters and catalysts in the change process in their respective communities. The program believes that learning can best happen within the sphere of the real world, through individual problem-posing. The instructional design focuses learners toward their real-world concerns. As part of this process, the facilitators of the learning experience validate participants' past experiences. They acknowledge that each individual is important in solving his or her community problems, as opposed to reliance on external experts (M. Harris, personal communication, July 1989).

In the world of corporate business, the IBM Management Development Center, at Armonk, New York, is focused on developing corporate leadership founded on the specific IBM beliefs of (1) respect for the individual, (2) commitment to excellence, and (3) importance of quality customer service. The development center is viewed as neutral, supportive territory for company employees; this perception is important because participants are selected from all segments of the corporation and sometimes are concerned about their acceptance in relation to individuals from other segments of the company. The physical and psychological environment has been designed to isolate participants from daily work issues or other external concerns, to stimulate socialization focused on the development of the group, and to provide an alcohol-free environment. The center, located next to corporate headquarters, was designed to be convenient for top IBM internal executives to participate in, so that in each program "future leaders could hear from the current company leaders." The center was designed as a total living-learning environment that supports the IBM company culture with quality adult learning experiences (T. Schappert, personal communication, July 1989).

Each learning sanctuary, including the two previous examples, has a specific "learning culture" reflected in the design of the facility and in its master educational plan. These cultural values of learning are both explicit and implicit in the setting. The two examples reflect highly focused centers and programs. Yet they, as well as most learning sanctuaries, serve diverse people, with some also serving multiple groups with different program concerns at the same time. This diversity could be troublesome for development and implementation of a learning culture. However, each learning sanctuary represents the key overarching elements of its own definition of a learning culture, no matter the size or complexity of the environment. For learning sanctuaries housed in universities and colleges, the learning culture often reflects a grounding in the "vision of the educated person," given by the liberal-arts and sciences traditions, and often based on the idea of dissemination of new research and theory. For voluntary associations and businesses, the sanctuary often reflects the specific tenets and belief systems of the organization, and the importance of group cohesion, organizational advancement, and development of knowledge and skills relevant to the organization. In all learning sanctuaries, the learning culture is based on the dignity of the adult learner and the importance of learning that is supported, challenged, and transformed through a process of environmental immersion.

The Dynamic of an Experiential Process. A master plan for a learning sanctuary is, in part, based in the necessity for the active, challenging involvement of adult learners. Clearly, adult participation in any learning experience is a given, often defined by traditional question-and-answer sessions or concurrent sessions for individual preference. However, the meaning of this experiential process goes beyond these normal adult instructional involvements. In contemporary society, there is a growing number of sophisticated and knowledgeable adult learners. Education programs that are designed in an overly conforming or constricting manner have an inhibiting, if not deadening, impact. Many adult learners have developed complex and knowledgeable beliefs, a special set of "value lenses," regarding effective, stimulating, and challenging educational programs. Many have become part of a number of frequent attendees who speak of the boredom caused by the simplistic and almost childish expectations made by many residential education programs. This second element of the master plan suggests that educational planners must continually be innovators of forms, structures, and processes for adult learning.

This element of the master plan, the *dynamic of an experiential process*, suggests two key elements for program planners to consider. The first is the active involvement of the adult learner in "experiences" that provide both new information and learner actions to consider, test, and reflect on this information. Second, the program planner should acknowledge the organic development of a learner group, and of each learner, as they journey through the program. Due to the uniquely intensive nature of residential educational experiences, there should be a built-in dynamic, a synergy, within and between individuals. A residential experience has an internal unplanned dynamic that needs to be understood and, insofar as is possible, orchestrated by the instructional planners. During active engagement, learners, both as individuals and as group members, incorporate, modify, and create new learning interactions. Residential program planners should pay particular attention to these process elements that support and also challenge the "planned instructional program." Each set of circumstances, learner commitments, and group influences will dictate creative possibilities.

As one example of this dynamic, the Museum Management Institute is a unique four-week residential program for mid-career museum professionals. Offered at the University of California, Berkeley, the program design creates a "cultural island" to provide a catalyst for self-reflection of a personal and professional nature. In particular, participants examine the image and reflect on the past, present, and future of their sponsoring institutions. This executive-development program expects each participant to thoughtfully consider contexts of the individual, of the society, and of the museum and to reflect on the relationship of the museum professional to those contexts. The daytime core program presents an instructional content design integrating adult teaching strategies. However, this core content is only one aspect of the program; the planners assume that the residential experience should encompass the learners throughout their stay. For example, each evening there is a focused group interaction, called a fireside chat. In this gathering, one of the institute's instructional leaders discusses a specific philosophical issue, such as how a predominantly Anglo-based museum culture can present and reflect other cultures in a sensitive and authentic way. Each week of the institute features a live-in senior mentor who comes from a different type of museum experience (art, history, science, and technology). This senior mentor not only participates in the daily instructional activities but is also available after hours for personal and small-group consultations. The adult and continuing educational program leader also provides consultation throughout the four-week period on personal and professional matters of interest to the adult learner. In addition, as the group identifies key concerns and issues that need "expertise," the program can fly in experts on specific topics during the four-week institute. Thus, the learning agenda of the program can incorporate new group-identified needs and interests (P. Nowlen, personal communication, July 1989).

Beyond experiential opportunities for current learner's pursuits, the learning sanctuary should provide a bridge between the learner and new research, techniques, and technologies. Given the rapid growth of information and technology, the residential experience is a prime candidate to introduce and provide learner opportunities for exploration of such areas. For example, a learning sanctuary could stimulate learner use and understanding of newer technologies, such as access to special video channels or libraries, use of computers both inside and outside class, and, for more knowledgeable and sophisticated users, the ability to modem-access broader library and data-base information sources. For example, a number of university residential conference centers now have available, as planned or optional programming, computer-related activities through simulation games, use of specific professional computer packages, or data-base access.

As another example, IBM has an advanced-technology classroom designed for adult experiential involvement. Each adult participant has an instructional workstation in the classroom featuring a personal computer with a laser touch screen for immediate feedback to individual participants. The instructor has a remote control device to manipulate videotape, videodisc, and other technological devices, based on group and instructor learning agendas. All instruction in this setting assumes a maximum of a fifteen-minute lecture followed by a focused segment on learner-active participation and involvement. In the student's private living area, closed circuit TV is available with continuously playing videotapes on various topical areas of management, personnel issues of mental health, stress, and personal development. In addition, IBM will be incorporating personal computer hook-ups in the living facilities for participation in out-of-class learning experiences (T. Schappert, personal communication, July 1989). The Xerox International Center for Training and Management Development in Leesburg, Virginia, has dedicated over 111,000 square feet to laboratory facilities in the belief that most of their technical training should be in the laboratory, should be "technology-driven," and should be the most current, if not futuristic. Thus, for their service training, participants spend one hour in class for every seven hours in the laboratory. With this dedicated facility, the latest in technology is available to the learner for full-access and experiential, intensive involvement (W. Zawacki, personal communication, July 1989).

Holistic Involvement of the Learner. Each learning sanctuary reflects a belief in the holistic involvement of the learner in both active and passive learning. This involvement is often narrowly defined through active teaching-learning strategies (in large part discussed in the above section). But also there should be a focus on active involvement of the body and the soul, as well as the mind. Program planners should be concerned with forms of physical activity and exercise, of "wellness." In addition, the learner often brings a desire to embrace aesthetic dimensions of an environment, either through art, music, dance, or interests reflecting philosophical and historical concerns. The learner carries a set of values, ethics, and meanings that are also actively embraced and considered during this process. Planners should be mindful of these elements in the design and implementation of the program. For example, the learning sanctuary can reaffirm or create greater awareness of the learner's cultural identity and values in light of the new and changing world encountered in the sanctuary. At Highlander Center, they request that individuals bring musical instruments for evening gatherings to share Appalachian folk music and story telling. These events provide an important role in individuals' "reidentifying and reaffirming their own culture and community" (M. Harris, personal communication, July 1989).

Equally important to holistic involvement are the passive aspects of an adult learner's experience in a residential environment. These passive aspects provide an important life balance and often are of greater significance than active aspects for certain learner styles. Passive opportunities offer a calming and renewing of energy, opportunities for reflection on personal perspectives, and support for self-directed pursuits focused in individual goals for learning. They allow learners to psychologically remove themselves from an immediate experience and ease the tensions that come from intense involvement in learning. But of greater significance, these passive times are critical to the well-being of the learner. The "whole learner" is not a cerebral being. The body and the spirit of the learner should be attended to through interpersonal exchange, relaxation, and rest. These moments are vital for individuals to renew and revitalize themselves, to critically contemplate personal meanings, to analyze their mental perspectives, and to consider the future of their lives.

This key element of a "holistic learning culture" with its active and passive aspects can be seen in two varied residential experiences. As one example, consider the nature of educational program planning for religious organizations within a retreat or conference facility. Camp Junaluska, a Methodist age-integrated residential facility in North Carolina, provides diverse educational programming focused on the whole person within the religious experience. This center, serving up to a maximum of 2,000 people, attempts to integrate programming focused on spiritual development and renewal, on creation of a "temporary Christian community" through fellowship and community building, and on development of individual competence in specific group educational activities.

Beyond these fundamental goals of the camp, individual activities (called adjunct programming) are offered to serve the unique, personal needs of participants. As part of these efforts, they focus on the importance of the physical well-being of participants through a fitness center, called the Wealth Center. As with many fitness centers, this one features group and individual learning experiences designed to improve, develop, and maintain physical fitness and well-being. They also offer individuals an opportunity to consider the past tradition of the spiritual community through a United Methodist Heritage Center (a historical museum) and to consider the individual's future development through access to instructional and conference staff as well as to the "portable resources" of a library and a bookstore. They assume that individuals come with specific learning agendas, some of which can be fulfilled through the group instructional experience, the religious experience, and community fellowship experiences. Other individual needs can be potentially addressed through their Intentional Growth Center. This center at the camp offers individual self-directed learning experiences of either guided professional and personal enhancement (such as time-management or leadership skills) or of spiritual development (such as a specialized course in spiritual formation). In addition, the location of the camp in the mountains gives individuals and groups a chance to draw on its natural setting and isolation for important opportunities for individual self-examination, reflection, and meditation (R. Ponder, personal communication, July 1989).

Professional adult and continuing educators can use the program structure to stimulate adult participants' critical reflections on their current professional and personal lives. These possibilities are often brought to learners' minds through activities that bridge the learners' perspectives and the concerns of their daily world with individual or group problem-solving in the learning environment. The Museum Management Institute uses a case-study method to gain both the active and passive problem-solving involvement of the learner. Part of this instructional focus is a major assignment for each participant, which is started prior to entry into the institute program. Each individual is sent selected readings and a preparatory assignment. Participants must bring to the institute a draft statement of (1) the mission of their museum and (2) the outline of a specific problem or a special issue that they wish to consider during the institute session. Through the four weeks of residential involvement, individuals are expected to consider their case problem in light of the seminars given. On the third week, each working group selects one of the group member's problems that is particularly rich in issues and concerns. The group becomes a consulting team to the individual with the case problem. Working as a team, they make significant efforts (often after-hours and on weekends) to critique the problem definition, to consider multiple issues and strategies posed by the problem, and to produce a set of recommendations. This process significantly aids individuals in developing new ways to define and resolve problems, as well as helping them develop skills in learning and consulting with other key museum professionals. This process also has both active and passive interaction, helping participants learn about their own questions and perspectives in relation to other members of the group (P. Nowlen, personal communication, July 1989).

The Learning Sanctuary and Self-Directed Learning Pursuits. The learning sanctuary should not only support the key program goals of the formal classroom educational experience. It should provide a bridge to self-directed learning pursuits. A learning sanctuary is cognizant that adults do not learn solely within a group-program context. Therefore, the sanctuary should provide a rich menu of advocacy, opportunities, models, and resources for participants' personal learning needs. These opportunities are often indigenous to the particular setting of the center. Some residential centers can draw on urban environments and their diversity of cultural institutions; others can incorporate access to the rich resources of their parent universities. All centers can create structures and opportunities as well as capitalize on their natural and cultural surroundings.

A number of residential conference centers have systematically developed "in-house" resources as well as structured experiences for participant self-directed learning pursuits. By providing specific program resources and consultant expertise, a learning sanctuary can effectively provide another layer of learning experience for the participant. In this way, a learning sanctuary can acknowledge the importance of individual learning. Many of the above examples of residential adult education have highlighted the integration of individual learning needs, self-directed learner resources, and focused program components for individual learning pursuits.

In recognition of the importance of self-directed learning as the cutting edge for innovation in residential settings, a number of programs and centers have created special resource rooms, specialized individual guided learning resource experiences, and access to video and computer instructional experiences. For example, one institution is experimenting with a model of self-directed learning as its program focus. The Georgia Center for Continuing Education at the University of Georgia is currently designing an instructional program targeted to individual learners who desire to explore their roles as ethical decision-makers. This course would be oriented to self-directed learners who desire to explore individually their own learning agendas concerning ethical decision-making. After a preliminary background information exchange, learners would receive specific readings and guided instructional materials, prior to entry to the Georgia Center. Upon beginning their self-directed learning experience, they would be guided as independent learners through their self-identified learning experiences. As part of this program, participants could utilize the center's resource-center library and other resources from the university environment and would interact with specifically designated topic-area faculty mentors regarding learning goals and learning concerns that the participants have themselves defined. In addition, group interaction with other self-directed learners in this "self-directed program" would be provided through informal group gatherings and meal-time conversations. It is hoped that this experimental model would aid the participants to better understand themselves and their role as ethical decision-makers, as well as aid their reflections on the context of ethical decisions and actions in the contemporary world (E. Simpson, personal communication, July 1989).

According to a different perspective regarding self-directed learning and its relationship to a residential experience, the Federal Aviation Administration's Center for Management Development in Palm Coast, Florida, assumes that its mission encompasses serving learners both on-site and at distant work sites. In addressing workplace issues and "effective tactics to foster positive employee relations," the center provides a resource center with an on-site library, individualized study courses, and computer-based instruction. It also offers a nonresidential program for employees who are unable to attend residential classes (*CMD Review*, 1988).

Conclusion

An effective learning sanctuary program reflects these four components: a learning culture, holistic learner involvement, a dynamic experiential process, and self-directed learning. These elements occur because an expert program planner with the residential instruction and housing staff designed and implemented a specific psychological and environmental residential educational experience. As pointed out in the research of Kafka and Griffith (1984), "In the final analysis, it is the expertise of the program planner in utilizing the potential for control of the learning environment, and not simply the physical characteristics of residential conference centers, that determines the relative effectiveness of residential adult education" (p. 25). It is not the placement of an educational experience within a residential format that is the key. The *residential education process,* rather than an education-in-residence, is

> a total experience in which the academic and social activities are integrated through a conscious process of living together as a group, and the factor of residence is central rather than peripheral to the education achieved [Siegle, 1956, p. 108].

Residential education in a learning sanctuary is a carefully planned, multiple-day experience in a living-learning educational setting. A learning sanctuary goes beyond a traditional residential experience by presenting a "learning culture," a learning environment that incorporates adult learners' commitment, involvement, and growth. It reflects a more complex and thoughtful master plan, utilizing both the facilities and the human resources of the residence center. It reflects deep concern for each learner as an adult, as a member of a learning group, and as an individual investing in a highly personal and transforming learning experience.

References

Bruner, J. S. *Beyond the Information Given.* New York: Norton, 1973.
CMD *Review*, 1988, *1* (1), (entire issue). (Available from Center for Management Development, Attention: Editors, *CMD Review*, 4500 Palm Coast Parkway East, Palm Coast, Fla. 32037.)

Collins, M. "Quality Learning Through Residential Conferences." In P. Ilsley (ed.), *Improving Conference Design and Outcomes.* New Directions for Continuing Education, no. 28. San Francisco: Jossey-Bass, 1985.

Gardner, J. W. *Self-Renewal.* New York: Harper & Row, 1964.

Houle, C. O. *Residential Continuing Education.* Notes and Essays on Education for Adults, no. 70. Syracuse, N.Y.: Syracuse University, 1971.

"How Do We Learn?; How Do We Teach?; How Do Learners Retain?" Socony-Vacume Oil Company Studies, n.d.

Kafka, J. J., and Griffith, W. S. "Assessing the Effectiveness of Residential Adult Education." *Continuum,* 1984, 48 (1), 19–26.

Knowles, M. S. *The Modern Practice of Adult Education: From Pedagogy to Andragogy.* New York: Cambridge, The Adult Education Company, 1980.

Siegle, P. E. "The International Conference on Residential Adult Education." *Adult Education,* 1956, 7 (2), 108–109.

Carol E. Kasworm is associate professor of adult education at the University of Tennessee, Knoxville. She was editor of Education Outreach to Select Adult Populations *and has directed and consulted on residential learning program designs and facilities.*

Researchers have demonstrated that conference center environmental design significantly affects a person's psychological comfort.

Environmental Psychology of the Learning Sanctuary

James P. Pappas

"It's good to be back in Mecca."
—Comment by a participant returning
to a residential center

"I think I saw a cockroach in my room. If I see it again, I'm going to demand my money back."
—Comment by a participant
at a residential center

The environment of a residential conference center, in terms of time and place, has a unique set of meanings for its program participants. Too often, continuing education programmers forget to consider how potent the center's environment itself can be on nontraditional learners. When attention is drawn to this potency we are quick to give lip service to it. However, there is seldom sufficient time and energy directed to enhancing the environmental impact of a residential center.

The metaphor of the learning sanctuary suggests that the physical facilities and the psychological environment of a residential center should make a significant difference in the learning experience. Past research in environmental psychology has clearly demonstrated that a person's behavior and attitude can be influenced by specific aspects of a physical setting or by a person's perceptions of an environment. The present chapter will draw on this research in environmental psychology and suggest key findings that can be directly applied to a residential continuing education center. This exploration will include a discussion of spatial behavior, an appraisal of physical characteristics of meeting rooms and classrooms, a

NEW DIRECTIONS FOR ADULT AND CONTINUING EDUCATION, no. 46, Summer 1990 © Jossey-Bass Inc., Publishers discussion of the role of tradition, and an analysis of how a participant anticipates and responds to an environment. The last section will present an outline for action that will identify key findings that can be applied to the practice of residential education.

Key Elements of a Psychological Environment

Virtually any and all aspects of the physical environment can have special psychological meaning to an individual. As suggested earlier, these meanings are often idiosyncratic or personal. However, there have now been a sufficient number of studies conducted for data to emerge that allow generalization regarding some of the following elements.

Spatial Behavior

Adults have a perceived sense of space or territory in relation to their social interactions and in relation to their sense of comfort within physical space. This concept of spatial behavior in environmental psychology has been among the most broadly researched concepts, with well over seven hundred studies (Aiello, 1987). As Sommer (1969) has said, spatial behavior is a little like the porcupine in Schopenhauer's fable: People like to be close enough for warmth and comradeship but far enough away to avoid pricking each other.

People appear to maintain a small protected psychological sphere or "bubble" between themselves and others. It is in this area immediately surrounding individuals where most interactions with others take place; anyone who enters this space and is not perceived as welcome becomes an "intruder." As noted by Hall (1969) and validated by more recent research, there are four zones of defined spatial behavior. Intimate distance ranges from zero to eighteen inches and is characterized by strong and intense sensory inputs. Personal distance ranges from one and a half to four feet and is more likely to be used by friends and acquaintances. Social distance, for more formal and businesslike transactions, extends from four to twelve feet. The last zone, public distance, extends beyond twelve feet and is primarily used for either communication functions (public groupings) or for protective functions (interactions with negative public behaviors).

As one might suspect, there appear to be gender and cultural differences in the use of interpersonal distance (Aiello and Aiello, 1974; Tennis and Dabbs, 1975; Patterson and Schaeffer, 1977). A predominant finding in this area is that males use more interaction space than females (Fisher and Byrne, 1975; Hughes and Goldman, 1978) and that people in the "contact cultures," such as southern Europeans, Latin Americans, and Arabs, maintain closer interaction distances and exhibit a higher amount of involvement with each other when interacting than do northern Europeans and North Americans (Aiello, 1987).

Another variable that seems to affect the use of spatial behavior is personality traits (Mehrabian and Diamond, 1971; Wormith, 1981). Individuals who have higher self-esteem or who are less neurotic are more likely to use more space but are also more willing to allow others to approach them closer. As one would predict, those higher in affiliation needs have a tendency to sit closer to others and intrude more often. Also, the need to control leads to greater space utilization.

Given these research findings, most practitioners in conference centers observe adults effectively utilizing physical space when it does not inhibit their sense of social interaction. Thus, residential conference facilities should provide reasonably sized spaces, rather than smaller spaces, for interaction; participants, when given sufficient space, will create their own groupings within the space, based on personal needs. Most residential conference facilities provide alcoves and furniture arrangements that take into account environmental barriers but also offer diversity in the interior setting of the facility. Cavernous or sterile meeting areas often alienate participants. Also, the general meeting areas as well as instructional facilities are often created with seating arrangements in circular or open forms that allow for greater eye and expressive contact. This arrangement does stimulate greater participant interaction. When making room and seating arrangements as well as identifying space for social interaction, residential conference planners should remember the porcupine allusion. Simply stated, you are more concerned if you are crowded too close than if you are seated too far apart. Second, spatial arrangements are more easily identified and perceived in similar ways by participants who have affiliated membership or have similar characteristics.

Physical Characteristics of the Environment and Their Impact
There has been considerable writing in the public media (most of it subjective) describing "good" and "bad" environmental design for meeting rooms, sleeping accommodations, and building plans. Environmental psychologists are much less clear as to what is and what is not an appropriate environmental design. This is because each individual has a different learning history about what is and what is not an effective response to sounds, temperatures, colors, and other sensory aspects of the environment. A number of other variables—such as ongoing activity, the social or group environment, the opportunity for adaptation, the nature of the overall building environment, and participants' personalities—all seem to have an impact on these sensory aspects. Given this limitation, however, a number of researchers are discovering some norms that can at least guide environmental designers and programmers as they consider these variables in altering a conference environment. These variables are outlined below.

Light. One of the areas catching researchers' attention has been the effect of light on various work, office, and classroom situations (Chaikin,

Darlega, and Miller, 1976; Gifford, 1988; Sommer, 1974). One important variant is sun or natural light versus artificial light. There is accumulating evidence that sunlight has a tendency to improve mood much more than even bright artificial light. It is speculated that sunlight is preferred because its spectral distribution is quite different from that of artificial light. Normal individuals in work settings, psychiatric patients, and even animals appear to have a preference for natural lighting. Environmental design often requires the choice between having large windows to provide natural light or enduring the distractions that such open visual areas cause; yet there continue to be increasing arguments for the positive emotional effects of natural light. The problem of distractions can be controlled by higher placement of windows and effective blinds.

Additionally, there appear to be much data suggesting that brighter light of any type has a tendency to be more positively related to effective meetings and work tasks. As one looks at the specific behavioral outcomes of group conversation, interpersonal communication, and personal content of communication, brighter light does seem to foster such behavior. Gifford (1988), in studies at the University of Victoria, British Columbia, evaluated some of these variables and found that brighter lights tend to encourage more general and more intimate communication. These findings emerged even after he initially hypothesized that while bright light would cause more conversation it would be less effective than intimate lighting for personal and intimate conversation.

One aspect of the lighting effect is the impact of color on individuals. This again indicates the notion that spectral distribution of light may have a psychological impact on the mood of participants. Emerging data have confirmed that people prefer "cool" colors (blues and greens) over "warm" colors (reds and yellows) (Sundstrom, 1981). Further, people rate long wave length colors as more arousing than short wave length colors. For instance, red light appears to create greater arousal than does green. Many conference center directors and programmers have known intuitively that well-lighted, cool-colored rooms seem to be preferred by conference attendees. This is now being confirmed by environmental research.

Temperature. Most of the research conducted on effective temperature has been limited to work settings. Assuming generalizations may be made from this work-setting research, the findings can suggest trends or guidelines for conference planners, with the caveat again that this is another example of a subjectively experienced variable.

In broad-based studies, there does appear to be a temperature range that is acceptable to a majority of individuals. Harris and Associates (1980) reported that 81 percent of a sample of U.S. office workers found the ideal temperature to be between 68 and 73 degrees Fahrenheit (F), while only about 19 percent found this temperature range too warm or too cool. The median "ideal" temperature was found to be about 71 degrees F; only about

8 percent felt this to be too warm or too cold. On balance, the research suggests that high temperatures are more disruptive than cool temperatures. Given the nature of worker preferences and laboratory studies, it appears that conference planners can accept the common wisdom that room temperatures should be in the 71 to 72 degrees Fahrenheit range. At these temperatures, one can expect greater report of comfort and vigilance to tasks and mental activities.

Noise. Noise is generally defined as any unwanted sound and is one of the most intensely studied aspects of physical working environments (Kryter, 1970; Harris and Associates, 1980). If one looks at the effects of noise in office or general work situations, noise appears to be one of the most prevalent problems reported as interfering with participant and worker effectiveness. In a survey of office workers, over 49 percent complained about the lack of quiet in their offices (Harris and Associates, 1980). Interestingly, and of relevance to conference settings, among the most distracting or annoying types of noise were conversations by other workers and ringing of telephones, the former because one has a tendency to try to listen and the latter because it forces one to determine who is being called. Similar studies in public school settings suggest similar findings.

A related variable is *music*, which was once thought to create a positive ambient environment and boost the morale of people listening to it. There have been no data to confirm strongly the idea that work output increases if music is played. However, there have generally been positive responses to survey data on the effectiveness of music in office or work areas— especially where there is other competing noxious noise (for example, keypunch-room noise, discussions at hotel front desks). Additionally, for low-level mental tasks, music seems to facilitate arousal, which positively affects vigilance and routine responses. In these studies, it should be noted, the music tends to be of low intensity and primarily instrumental with low demand characteristics. However, once the noise level reaches 100 decibels or more, these findings start to reverse.

Decor and Furniture Arrangement. As with other physical characteristics studies, most research has been related to work situations, although some studies have been carried on in public schools and college environments. In studies of work environments, it is evident that workstations and the space available for workstations have positive or negative effects on productivity and performance. People involved in mental tasks perform better if they have a large amount of floor space available, and satisfaction is dramatically increased (in a linear fashion) as the amount of floor space is increased, at least up to 100 square feet.

While little research has been conducted on specific furniture design, there has been some analysis of the effect of chairs. This has led to an entire field of furniture ergonomics and human-factors research. A problematic aspect of this research has been its equivocal nature and that it is susceptible to individual differences, particularly regarding the participant's size and weight. Sommer (1969), in his critical text on the subject, argues against the view that better work occurs in a straight-back chair, either in the case of an employee or a student. His views have generally been confirmed by research (Ayoub, 1973; Kleeman, 1981; Woodson, 1981). Considerable evidence exists to suggest that workers, students, and meeting participants are more productive if the chair is *perceived* as comfortable; comfort being most often defined as cushioned chairs with armrests (Harris and Associates, 1980).

A related variable studied to some degree is *room decor.* Gifford (1988)—following the work of Maslow and Mintz (1956); Chaikin, Darlega, and Miller (1976); and Sommer (1974)—conducted a study to see if decor enhanced interpersonal communication and discussions. He compared the level of communication in a room with typical modern office furniture (for example, armless molded plastic chairs and standard tables) with a similar room featuring virtually the same furniture (except for padded arm chairs) but personalized by potted plants, framed art posters on the wall, and small decorative rugs and lamps. Measures of concern included conversation, self-referent words, and intimacy on eleven topics. Results showed that the decor significantly affected the general level and intimacy of the communication. The overall conclusion was that the general and interpersonal nature of communication in a setting could be increased by more personal and comfortable decor.

The Role of Tradition

Beyond considerations of the physical characteristics of a setting, administrators of a residential learning environment should be aware of the significance of tradition as it influences the perceptions and behaviors of adult participants. Jacobi and Stokols (1983) suggest that the physical setting has an important role in determining the scope, quality, and intensity of transactions between persons and their environment. In analyzing the subjective links between people and places, Jacobi and Stokols found that there are two critical elements in the way people view any environmental setting and its relationship to events that occur there. These elements are the concept of *place identity* (its properties) and the *symbolic nature of the place as it relates to the self* (for example, how a participant identifies with the setting). Thus, the physical environment and the events of a residential educational program can acquire emotional and symbolic value for the individual. The environment and program can also take on a unique capacity to evoke vivid, widely held social meanings in all of the participants; they can become a tradition that is part of an organizational culture, or they can have specific psychological meanings and establish expectations for participants when they return to the center or when they discuss the past experience of this tradition with others.

The classic example of the role that tradition plays is a university setting, which derives a sense of tradition from its physical design, age, history, and educational orientation and from the added experiences of students and faculty. Business and industry residential training facilities, as well as nonprofit association and religious educational facilities, also blend within their settings images of organizational culture and history, special programs, or facility rituals and traditions. The traditions of a residential center are influenced through program design, services, and the specific experiences of participants and instructors. The role of tradition is an important element in understanding the impact of a residential learning experience. The opening epigraph of this chapter quoted a participant who felt he was "returning to Mecca" when he came back for his third and final session at a one-week-per-year institute. His use of symbolic language for the conference center and program reflects the potency of a setting, of a meaningful program, and of a learning-sanctuary experience.

The Affective Experience

Conference participants relate to a living-learning environment from an emotional as well as a cognitive base. Occasionally an emotion can be direct—especially for a negative condition. As an example, the second epigraph for this chapter is a clear and easily discernible affective response. More often, participant perceptions of the environment tend to be intermingled, with the strongest affective experiences usually voiced by the participant. As suggested by Russell and Snodgrass (1987),

> When you arrive [at a place], you are likely to be struck by [its] affective quality. . . . Affective quality is the bottom line of an accounting of the many features in a place, and is, we believe, a guide for much of your subsequent relationship to that place—what to do there, how well it is done, how soon to leave, whether or not to return. Afterward, you often remember little more about a place than its affective quality: [In fact] behavior may be influenced by the (estimated, perceived, or remembered) affective quality of an environment rather than its objective properties directly [p. 253].

Ordinarily, when participants affectively evaluate conferences and conference centers, the setting and the specific educational program events are relatively well defined. Thus, the continuing educator should be aware that participant reports of excitement, happiness, pleasure, boredom, or hostility to their experience directly reflect on the setting and the program. Consequently, continuing education programmers should be aware that they are seeking to direct or alter moods, that is, the affective quality of the participants' experience in the learning sanctuary.

Participants' Experience of a Residential Conference

Having considered research on influential psychological aspects of an environment, we should also consider how the individual participant approaches, participates in, and leaves a conference center on completing a program. At the core of these concerns is the participant's *subjective plan* of what he or she anticipates will happen at a conference. A few years ago Berne and his associates (1964) suggested that, in responding to events, we all consciously or unconsciously follow a series of "scripts." Current environmental psychologists now term this concept an "affective plan." While different for each individual, this plan may be outlined as follows:

Step One: Before Entering the Environment. Before entering a place, the individual has typically planned to go there and planned what he or she will do while there—though for some, the plan may be quite vague (Russell and Snodgrass, 1987). The first sequence of the plan is receiving information. In the case of conferences, participants may receive a conference brochure, review its contents, assume that it is helpful to his or her professional life, and make a perhaps flawed determination that the quality and attractiveness of the brochure imply the quality and attractiveness of the conference. From negative to neutral to positive, participants will experience an array of feelings about the conference location and about the travel required to reach the location. They may then make an initial decision to do further planning.

Mayo and Jarvis (1981) and Stokols and Novaco (1981) have examined the role of travel in a variety of environment-related activities. As one would expect, as time and distance increase to arrive at an event, the potential for difficulties or a negative response also increases. This is particularly true for professional people, who tend to be highly task- and demand-oriented. Travel presents stress and pressures, with the potential for conflict in schedules and work commitments.

Other elements that are part of the first step are adaptation level and expectation. These obviously affect the individual attending a conference. If, for example, an academic conference is slated for mid-September when most participants tend to be hassled by registration at the beginning of their academic year, we may have already predisposed those participants to a negative response. Further, if we have our conference in a very busy urban or metropolitan city where travel from the airport is particularly expensive and difficult, the likelihood of a negative response is increased, especially if most of the participants are coming from small towns or rural environments. Finally, if the brochure content is not replicated in the conference program, then further deterioration of response is likely to follow.

Step Two: Effects of the Environment. While in the environment, the content of the program and social group will clearly make a difference. But within the context outlined above, it should be recognized that sensory experiences such as architecture, color, decor, and temperature as well as psychological variables such as spacing and tradition will all affect the response. Various features are mixed together in the mind of the participant to create the environmental sense he or she will take away from the conference. There is also an array of additional physical features that affect the way he or she experiences the conference and the conference center. These could include such things as complexity, novelty, and meaning.

There is a tendency on the part of architects and building designers to create physical environments that are complex and seek to serve a number of purposes. As Wohlwill, Nasar, De Joy, and Foruzani (1976, p. 73) have said, "To sum it up, it is apparent that complexity, however much it might be touted by designers, plays an uncertain role at best in the individual's response to the environment." There is some indication that participants prefer easily understood and somewhat familiar environments if they are to be comfortable in a conference setting. One thing that appears to be consistent is that complex corridors, long distances between conference rooms and sessions, and poorly marked facilities all lead to negative moods. At the same time, if novelty does exist in appropriate amounts and within a context of familiarity, then the conference will probably receive a positive affective appraisal. For this reason, conference center designers should seek novelty in amenities (for example, statues, art work, fountains) and not in unique floor plans or building designs.

A third aspect of the affective environment relates to the meaning of a physical structure. Meaning, in this instance, relates to the consistency of a place with its history and traditional rituals and activities. Residential centers should have a logical compatibility with their surroundings. A high-rise, glitzy hotel in the middle of a rural campus composed primarily of one- and two-story buildings may have a negative effect, while the same structure in an urban university may be very logical.

A final aspect of environmental effects relates to how the environment either blocks or facilitates the individual participant's previously formulated plan. For example, if the conference is held in a center crowded with other conferences, if the rooms seem small and schoolroom like, and if the noise level is high and distracting, then the affective appraisal will certainly be low.

Step Three: The Effects of the Environment and Mood. We have described how a person arrives at a place and affectively appraises it as he or she attempts to carry out a plan to realize what was sought from the conference. That plan is either blocked or facilitated by the environment. As a result, an individual's mood may be altered, especially if there is a series of negative events that disrupt expectations. In true psychological fashion, this can lead to basic emotions of flight or fight. Flight can be either immediate or relate to future conferences. Fight is often demonstrated with numerous complaints and negative evaluations. With more knowledgeable conference attendees, negative physical amenities will lead conference instructors and planners to attempt to alter the conference design by starting informal sessions or seeking to preempt conference schedules for other activities. Sometimes this can be "healthy." However, if too much of it occurs during a conference, one should use that as a clue that something is gravely wrong.

Step Four: After-Effects. Leaving a place does not, of course, end its influence. The mood created by the conference center can continue to influence behavior long after the sessions end. A conference often starts a series of psychological processes that, fueled by the emotion it has elicited, can affect the participants' lives positively or negatively. Typically, one would seek enthusiastic and satisfied conferees because this would lead to applications of the conference activities back home. Additionally, it would mean that the conferee carries back a positive recollection and will relate it to friends and prospective future participants.

While this arena of environmental psychology is still relatively new, the ascribing of mood and meaning to place and the examination of subjective plans of conferees promises to be the most significant aspect of understanding conference-center design. Conference planners and programmers should recognize these emotional responses and seek to manipulate the environment, the program, and the services to obtain a positive participant response.

An Outline for Action

Given the varied psychological elements that influence a participant's experience in a residential conference setting, it is hoped that conference planners and programmers will consider a wide variety of methods and strategies to enhance the impact of their programs. To encourage future consideration of this discussion, the following summary presents the key concepts and research findings from the literature on environmental psychology.

1. The environment (the conference center) is a critical component of a conferee's perception of the conference experience.

2. While the research in the field is equivocal, some emerging trends can be considered. In terms of critical person and environment variables we can say:

- Spatial behavior serves a protective and communicative function. A person seeks to create psychological space encompassing interactions and inhibiting intrusions. In conversations and seating behavior, people want expressive contact that controls who enters their life space. So they prefer alcoves, circular tables, and other similar furniture arrangements to open undefined space.

- Lighting seems to have a special effect on participant interaction. Natural or bright lights enhance general and intimate conversation and task performance.
- Most individuals prefer cool colors (blues and greens) to warm colors (reds and yellows).
- Most individuals prefer temperatures in the 71-to-72-degree F range.
- Noise can be among the most irritating distractors, especially if it involves abrupt or loud sounds or sound that demands attention (for example, nearby conversation, a ringing telephone).
- Participants prefer comfortable decor and furniture that allow interaction with all conferees. Circular arrangements with soft chairs are most desirable.
- Tradition, including the idea of place identity and symbolic relationship to the participant, is a critical variable.

An effective and successful residential learning experience must be based on a clean living space and a well-designed instructional program. Conference center planners should pay attention to how they create an attractive, inviting, and comfortable living-learning space for each participant.

References

Aiello, J. R. "Human Spatial Behavior." In D. Stokols and I. Altmaedn (eds.), *Handbook of Environmental Psychology*. New York: Wiley, 1987.

Aiello, J. R., and Aiello, T. D. "The Development of Personal Space: Proxemic Behavior of Children 6 Through 16." *Human Ecology*, 1974, 2, 177–189.

Ayoub, M. M. "Work Place Design and Posture." *Human Factors*, 1973, 15, 265–268.

Berne, E. *Games People Play*. New York: Grove Press, 1964.

Chaikin, A. L., Darlega, V. J., and Miller, S. J. "Effects of Room Environment on Self Disclosure in a Counseling Analog." *Journal of Counseling Psychology*, 1976, 23, 479–481.

Coyne, R. K., and Clark, R. J. *Environmental Assessment and Design*. New York: Praeger, 1981.

Fisher, J. D., and Byrne, D. "Too Close for Comfort: Sex Differences in Response to Invasions of Personal Space." *Journal of Personality and Social Psychology*, 1975, 32, 15–21.

Gifford, R. "Light, Decor, Arousal, Comfort and Communication." *Journal of Environmental Psychology*, 1988, 8, 177–189.

Hall, E. *The Hidden Dimension: An Anthropologist Examines Man's Use of Space in Public and Private*. Garden City, N.Y.: Anchor, 1969.

Harris, L., and Associates. *The Steelcase National Study of Office Environments No. 2*. Grand Rapids, Mich.: Steelcase, 1980.

Hughes, J., and Goldman, M. "Eye Contact, Facial Expressions, Sex and the Violation of Personal Space." *Perceptual and Motor Skills*, 1978, 46, 529–584.

Jacobi, M., and Stokols, D. "The Role of Tradition in Group Environment Relations." In N. R. Feimer and E. S. Geller (eds.), *Environmental Psychology: Directions and Perspectives*. New York: Praeger, 1983.

Kleeman, W. B. *The Challenge of Interior Design.* Boston: CBI, 1981.

Kryter, K. D. *The Effects of Noise on Man.* New York: Academic, 1970.

Maslow, A. H., and Mintz, N. L. "Effects of Esthetic Surroundings." *Journal of Psychology,* 1956, *41,* 247–254.

Mayo, E. J., and Jarvis, L. R. *The Psychology of Leisure Travel.* Boston: CBI, 1981.

Mehrabian, A., and Diamond, S. G. "Effects of Furniture Arrangements, Props and Personality on Social Interaction." *Journal of Personality and Social Psychology,* 1971, *20,* 18–30.

Patterson, M. L., and Schaffer, R. "Effects of Size and Sex Composition on Interaction Distance, Participation, and Satisfaction in Small Groups." *Small Group Behavior,* 1977, *8,* 433–442.

Russell, J. A., and Snodgrass, J. "Emotion and the Environment." In D. Stokols and I. Altman (eds.), *Handbook of Environmental Psychology.* New York: Wiley, 1987.

Sommer, R. *Personal Space: The Behavioral Bases of Design.* Englewood Cliffs, N.J.: Prentice-Hall, 1969.

Sommer, R. *Tight Spaces: Hard Architecture and How to Humanize It.* Englewood Cliffs, N.J.: Prentice-Hall, 1974.

Stokols, D., and Altman, I. (eds.). *Handbook of Environmental Psychology.* New York: Wiley, 1987.

Stokols, D., and Novaco, R. W. "Transportation and Well-Being: An Ecological Perspective." In I. Altman, J. F. Wohlwill, and P. B. Everett (eds.), *Transportation and Behavior.* New York: Plenum, 1981.

Sundstrom, E. *The Impact of Office Environment on Productivity and Quality of Life.* Buffalo, N.Y.: Bosti, 1981.

Tennis, G. H., and Dabbs, J. M., Jr. "Sex, Setting and Personal Space." *Sociometry,* 1975, *38,* 385–394.

Wohlwill, J. F., Nasar, J. J., De Joy, D. M., and Foruzani, H. H. "Behavior Effects on a Noisy Environment: Task Involvement Versus Passive Exposure." *Journal of Applied Psychology,* 1976, *61,* 67–74.

Woodson, W. G. *Human Factors Design Handbook.* New York: McGraw-Hill, 1981.

Wormith, J. S. "Personal Space of Incarcerated Offenders." *Journal of Clinical Psychology,* 1981, *40,* 815–827.

James P. Pappas is vice-provost for continuing education and public service at the University of Oklahoma. A clinical psychologist by training, he is also a professor of educational psychology.

Hospitality thoughtfully created within the residential center can provide a sense of security and well-being to the adult learner.

Creating an Atmosphere for the Learning Sanctuary

Roger E. Comley

Successful residential educational programs depend on carefully planned and managed environments because adult learners function best in a congenial atmosphere and an environment that provides a sense of security and well-being. Thus, the residential adult conference center, a planned learning environment, can provide the most effective setting for adult learning when operated with special sensitivity to social, psychological, and physical environmental factors.

Pappas, in Chapter Four, has provided an understanding of the environmental context of the residential center. This chapter will examine the residential center's supportive facilities and services as part of that environmental context. The support infrastructure of a learning sanctuary enhances or diminishes the adult learning experience. No matter how well conceived an instructional plan may be, the impact of well-maintained facilities and disciplined staff support makes a significant difference in the learner's attitude, involvement, comfort, and satisfaction. Without well-designed facilities for lodging, eating, and relaxation; without courteous and hospitable staff; and without streamlined operations supporting maintenance, cleaning, food service, accounting and billing, and guest services, a positive learning experience can be dramatically nullified.

A Matter of Philosophy

Administrators of facilities and of food and support services in residential conference centers are often perceived as the center's service providers, logistics experts, or fiscal managers. Although an effective service orientation and good business practices are important to maintain the economic viability of a residential center, its educational programs and the management of support services and facilities should be based on a philosophy of quality residential education. When a residential center functions as a learning sanctuary, it expresses, in many ways, the high priority given to learning by the center's administrators. The physical and social elements of a center reflect the values of those who control policy, funding, and management.

Conference centers, whether university-operated or entrepreneurial in nature, are not just physical structures and services. Whether for profit or not, they are educational environments that promote and support successful adult learning through their surroundings. An operating-services administrator for a residential conference center should believe that successful activities in the learning sanctuary rest on adherence to key principles in the effective management of educational programs. These principles, which are presented below, serve as the framework for guiding the planning and operation of the physical and support services found in the learning sanctuary. As such, they should provide the planning and action framework for all facility and support operations staff.

- Specify the highest possible quality in every aspect of conference-center operation and support services
- Respect the integrity of the conference center and never compromise its purposes as a sanctuary for learning
- Recognize that high standards of taste, refinement, and sophistication are required of the center
- Recognize that people are the principal ingredient in a center's successful operation
- Require that support services for an educational program of high quality be of equally high quality
- Respect the personal identity and importance of every individual.

Physical and Social Atmosphere

With the philosophical foundation for the learning sanctuary clearly in mind, we can now consider the ways in which the physical and social elements of the learning sanctuary contribute to effective adult education. Environmental surroundings, personal relationships, social events, and administrative processes are among the significant aspects of program planning to be considered.

Contribution of the Physical Environment. The learning sanctuary's facilities enhance educational processes in several ways. They illustrate and support the context and meaning of learning in an educational program; they promote interaction and exchange between the center's participants; they encourage both group and individual achievement; they contribute to the importance of individual identity; they reflect the bright and positive aspects of life; they generate optimism and hope; and they emphasize good taste and refinement. All of these possibilities are reflected in and supported by the nature, substance, and design of the center's physical facilities. The interior space, as well as the interior decoration of the center should be designed with consultation and advice from a professional designer. But the professional expertise of the educator should also be part of the consultative process. There should be a plan, reflecting the philosophy and spirit of the sanctuary, that relates human interaction to physical layout and interior design.

Hospitality and the Human Dimension. An environment is judged through the traditional five senses: sight, hearing, taste, smell, and touch. However, there is an important "sixth sense," meaning the emotional, affective judgment made of an environment; this sixth sense is that of *hospitality*. An operations administrator of a learning sanctuary should be focused on the way in which he or she communicates organizational values and the concept of hospitality. Hospitality is far more than an intention to extend courtesy and genuine warm feelings. It is comparable to the welcoming of guests to your home and making them feel that they belong there. Hospitality requires specific abilities, attitudes, and skills, and service is its principal ingredient. Good attitudes and pleasing appearances are essential in creating a hospitable impression. Interpersonal skills should be a high priority when selecting the staff of a center. Eagerness, sensitivity, finesse, and efficiency are powerful qualities in members of service organizations; these qualities set apart the best. The most successful conference centers are built on a foundation of carefully selected and well-trained staff, who create, through their orientation toward service, a strong feeling of hospitality.

Although the professional demeanor of a residential center often suggests a hospitable environment, professional and service staff are often unfamiliar with their own attitudes and actions as they reflect the feeling of hospitality that the center provides. An essential element of hospitality is recognizing the deep-set human need for individual recognition. Support staff should provide significant, ongoing recognition to conference participants. As a guideline, recognition of an individual's name is important, but with sensitivity to societal conventions. Generally, the use of first names (considered by some as presumptuous and discourteous) is reserved for friends and family. As part of establishing a professional and friendly environment, conference center staff strive to know and use last names (family names), with appropriate titles, when greeting conferees; first and last names are used when introducing them.

This recognition of the individual participant is a further challenge during the beginning stages of a residential program. Initial pleasant experiences reinforce the purposes of educational programs, while unpleasant experiences detract. In many instances, the first hours of a conference involve bringing together a number of individuals who frequently are total strangers. They are not only strangers but also represent differing regional cultures, ethnic and religious orientations, and sometimes languages. At first glance, these differences would seem to offer a complexity that detracts from the recognition of individuals and the development of a comfortable and secure learning environment. Both the program and operations staff should make specific plans to soften the somewhat austere atmosphere often created by these circumstances. Nevertheless, these circumstances offer an opportunity to add new dimensions of interest, varied educational experience, and excitement to the conference process.

Plans for receiving and introducing participants to the facility and to each other are an integral part of the program-planning process. Some educators, intent on jumping immediately into the deep waters of instruction, believe that a self-introduction ritual at the start of a program is sufficient. They begin with an exercise in which each participant presents himself or herself to the group. Often, however, the instructional situation makes this a practice of limited value. The center operations staff and instructional faculty should be trained to respond appropriately at their initial contacts with participants. They should have strategies, not only for knowing and using the last names of conference participants, but they should also actively introduce participants to one another. This should be a normal procedure during arrival of participants to the center, during the registration period, and also throughout the program. When a participant is recognized by name, his or her unique identity and individuality has been reinforced. Nothing is more personal and more at the core of effective hospitality than recognition of the individual.

Another essential element of hospitality focuses on the individual participant's need to experience a sense of security in the environment. Although most conference participants are relatively sophisticated travelers, few would admit to the insecurity experienced on arrival at a new destination. Actually, most adults view each new experience with some uncertainty. Everyone feels most secure when surrounded by supportive family, friends, and a familiar environment. Consequently, most of us are a bit off stride, insecure, and uncertain when adjusting to a new environment. While it is impossible to eliminate all insecurities, there are many elements of hospitality that can build feelings of trust and friendship. Security for the individual in a residential learning experience comes from friendly, helpful staff, as well as from well-maintained and physically secure facilities. Written and verbal communications that orient the conferee to various facilities, services, and assistance for specific needs reinforce feelings of security. Effective hospitality reflects the center's plan to "serve the adult" through individual recognition and establishment of a trust relationship that provides psychological and physical security. These considerations transform an unfamiliar environment that provides round-the-clock living services into a place of comfort and renewal. The learning sanctuary has an ambience that is receptive, reassuring, and secure; it feels good and is a good place in which to be.

Planning Effective Supportive Services in the Learning Sanctuary

There are certain critical aspects to be considered in conference management. Participants are generally arriving on unfamiliar ground and adjusting to new surroundings. Groups are often comprised of individuals who need to be carefully and properly introduced to one another. Conferences should include social activities and events planned with consideration to these needs. Human elements are central considerations in scheduling meetings and planning events. When sensitivity in planning is applied to these elements, the result is a measurably better conference.

Providing Effective Entry into the Center. On arrival, conferees should sense that they are expected. Many will arrive after long, tiring, and sometimes troublesome journeys; they may not be in the most pleasant frame of mind. Conference center staff should be organized to welcome, register, lodge, and orient the new arrivals. Efficient operation with minimal participant wait is the standard. Avoid cumbersome registration processes and bureaucratic rituals. Even those who arrive late at night should be provided prompt and courteous attention and provided as much assistance as possible.

Providing Decompression and Adjustment. Program planners should provide conferees with a period of rest prior to scheduling a social event, reception, or meal. This decompression time is welcomed by most conferees. When possible, the first segment of a residential education program should be a social event, unencumbered by an instructional exchange. Typically a residential educational program should begin during late afternoon or early evening to maximize the time for participant adjustment. This opening event should provide an informal setting to establish new relationships for conferees and acclimate them to new surroundings. During this event, the ambience and the support services are paramount to ensure a successful transition to the program.

What type of atmosphere and what elements should be considered in this first event? As one experiences this first coming together of strangers within an unfamiliar setting, the facilities and program staff should select a setting that is warm and inviting and that has been customized for this event. Signs of planning and special effort should be visible to the participants. Plants should be selected and placed in the room to soften corners and to add color. A large flower arrangement may dominate the center of the setting as the principal design feature, freshly arranged and coordinated with linen and background colors. Music is also an important component in establishing a hospitable and inviting atmosphere. Background music should be performed discretely below the level of conversation, with selections appropriate to the occasion and the audience. Food and beverages should be made easily available to the participants and thoughtfully selected for the time of day and nature of the gathering. Staff should be unobtrusive but efficient in handling the details of the event. These details of the initial entry and welcome to the center and to the program should reveal attentive planning and convey to the participant a sense of refinement, dignity, and personal importance. This initial event establishes identity between the participant and the program, center, and other participants. Conferees will begin their learning experience more reassured, relaxed, and confident.

Achieving Balance in the Conference Experience. Effective residential education conferences reflect a balance between social and instructional activity. Unfortunately, some educational program planners believe participants will not "get their money's worth" unless every available conference moment involves a structured delivery of subject matter. For example, group meals may be turned into planned discussion groups, and a banquet may become a setting for a major lecture.

"The banquet" should be a rewarding social experience. But often, overzealous planners use it to spotlight a "distinguished speaker." Harried participants who attempt to be gracious to a speaker while also meeting their own physical and social needs find actions incompatible and educationally ineffective. The program planner best serves the learning needs of the participants and provides the best learning environment for the "distinguished speaker" by separating the events. Also, participants react more positively to events that are clearly defined as either social or instructional.

Conference program meals have a meaningful and positive place in a residential educational experience. The group meal meets the practical need of providing attractive, nourishing food and beverage in a pleasant, refined setting without programs, instructions, or entertainment. The food, service, and hospitality are the centerpieces of the occasion. Relationships between participants are nurtured in a friendly atmosphere over good food, pleasantly served. These social times enhance receptivity and renew the minds of participants and, subsequently, the quality of participant interaction in the classroom.

Designing a Memorable and Meaningful Occasion. Most planners include at least one event within the conference that is unique and special. Such an event may be used to either open or close the conference, to recognize the accomplishments of presenters or participants, to present awards or certificates, to hear a keynote address, or to be entertained. Too often planners, thinking it efficient, try to include most of these purposes in one special event. Under the sheer weight of multiple purposes such occasions often collapse into boring, often exasperating, experiences for the participants.

The failure of a special event often comes from lack of planning and of sufficient resource support for implementation. Although important significance is assigned to the occasion, the objective of expressing that significance is often not effectively translated into reality. A common failure of the special event is the planner's attempt to schedule too much for too little time available. Another failure is to use the "banquet" as the stage for all the necessary but uninteresting aspects of the conference. Lengthy introductions and recognition programs might be better distributed among several meetings rather than imposed all at once on an unsuspecting banquet audience. Typically, the special event banquet is compromised until its main purpose becomes unclear.

The special event can be a truly meaningful occasion with memorable features. It deserves careful consideration for conference participants and understanding of the program's intent. There should be proper planning, and sufficient resources need to be provided. Planning should be done with the same thought and energy as is applied to any other aspect of the educational conference. The theme and purpose should be clearly determined and uncomplicated. If the "special session" is to be during a meal, then care should be taken in planning the meal and adequate time allowed to enjoy it. The purpose of the event may be conferee recognition, a thematic speech, or entertainment. However, the fulfillment of just one, good purpose should be sufficient.

The planning of special events is an art that requires an appreciation for integration of program and aesthetic concerns and an understanding of the related logistics. Cultural and artistic sensitivities need to be applied in determining the use of music, art, and entertainment as parts of the event. Combining a complex menu, a food-service plan, and a program requires intense preparation. Extensive logistical considerations are involved; however, the event can be presented without apparent concern or anxiety. Simplicity, efficiency, and professionalism are essential. Style and grace are products of good planning that effectively communicate the ambience of the learning sanctuary's environment. The specifics of what happened and what was served and said at the event may not be long remembered but the feeling created will endure.

Conference education planners do not need special ability in event planning, but they must appreciate and support its function and requirements. Facilities, food, and operations staff, working with educators, can provide expertise and coordinate planning for banquet management, service techniques, room decorating, color coordination, lighting, sound engineering, theatrical staging, and musical programming.

Addressing Client Diversity. Residential conference center programs often bring together participants from diverse cultural backgrounds. Staff must be sensitive to these cultural differences. In particular, this diversity must be acknowledged in the facilities, food services, instructional supports, and staff services. Successful program planners should avoid extremes in art, music, design, decoration, dining, entertainment, and literature. The environment communicates with each person, and any environmental statement that irritates a general audience is inappropriate. Cultural diversity can also be recognized as an element of the learning plan. For example, unique cultural experiences or artistic designs can be available elements in the teaching plan and may be part of the classroom experience. However, these presentations of a new or varied culture should be appropriate to the participant group and the event's circumstances.

The cultural diversity of participants should also be considered relative to kinds of facilities made available. Historically, fiscal austerity has dictated more spartan structures and interiors for campus-based conference centers, teaching facilities, and student housing quarters. However, these sometimes spartan environments are becoming less acceptable to adult clientele. Clients now have new and growing expectations for their living environment, food services, and comfort while learning. Returning to campus may have a nostalgic twist for some, but dormitory gang showers and college dining halls are becoming a part of the memories of youth.

Conference centers not associated with a university may look on their independent nature as a distinct advantage. However, many commercial centers have become oriented toward providing an atmosphere of glitz and opulence. Some are required to be revenue producers. Thus, the structure and support services, rather than the educational program, become the "main focus." These private operations should avoid overstatement and design extremes; they should avoid focusing solely on the financial side of the enterprise. Both private and university center operators need to pay more attention to the real needs—physical, social, educational—of their clientele. Facilities and services should be tailored to competitive considerations, but they should not lose sight of the center's educational mission.

Measuring Success. How can the residential administrative support staff members evaluate their success in providing a positive residential educational environment? Adults learn best when all support services are rendered at the highest level of quality. The gift of education is best received and retained when presented in an attractive package, wrapped in pleasant surroundings, and delivered with warm, sincere human feelings. Such a positive environment can be measured; evidence of it should be abundant and meaningful. At the conclusion of the program, participants should feel they have been personally enriched, as well as specifically improved through new knowledge. They should feel a sense of comfort in the environmental design; they should be relaxed and rejuvenated through the hospitable environment; they should be able to recall social moments and good personal experiences that were enhanced through the center's facilities, special events, and food and support services.

Three sources of information to measure success are suggested. The participants can respond to objective questions through end-of-program evaluation instruments. The staff of the conference center can also appraise the general disposition of the group. In particular, staff should solicit participant comments that critique as well as compliment. Lastly, the instructional staff and programmers will also note their own impressions and critical observations of the learning group, their entry and their exit as unique and changed people. The staff and programmers should reflect and evaluate not only the nature of these changes, including the specific impact of successful and unsuccessful events, but they should also consider the powerful environmental impacts on the group. Often an instructor's impression of group attitudes is an important indicator of environmental effect.

Creating the Standards for the Learning Sanctuary

If we genuinely believe in the learning sanctuary, we should accept the responsibilities of discipleship. These responsibilities focus on key philosophical tenets that undergird the learning sanctuary concept and that create an environment that holistically serves adult learners. These tenets should direct us in planning and decision making. By adhering to them, we are better able to create an environmental ambience, plan and organize programs and processes, and render support services that contribute to excellent learning experiences. These tenets are offered for final consideration:

• The highest possible quality is planned and specified for all support services. Resources are selected first according to need, without regard to cost. Decisions to use fewer resources are made only after the best possible resources are identified and it is clearly established that economic considerations make them unattainable. Alternative resources are then selected against this criterion of quality.

• The learning sanctuary, as defined, is always dedicated to education. Operating policies, practices, and procedures are developed that protect and preserve the integrity of its mission. No feature, facility, or service is either added or deleted without consideration of its relationship to adult education and its contribution to the environment. No activity is permitted within the environment that is inconsistent with the educational mission.

• Planning should be based on assumptions of good taste, refinement, and sophistication of clientele. These standards should compliment clientele and enhance the experiences of the entire educational process. Food, art, drama, music, and design are important expressions of life and reflect intrinsic educational value in the learning sanctuary.

• People are the most valuable component and most significant consideration in every aspect of management, operation, instruction, and process. High standards are used in the selection of personnel. A capacity to understand, support, and contribute to the philosophies of the learning sanctuary is expected of every staff member. This commitment and understanding should be part of the selection and of the training process of all personnel. As ethic and cultural diversity enriches the learning sanctuary, so does it contribute to the social environment. Interpersonal skills, human understanding, and cultural and ethnic diversity are critical personnel qualities to be sought and encouraged.

• The personal identity of every individual is respected. Processes and procedures are established to encourage individual recognition. Program participants are aware that, although a member of the group, each participant has an individual identity that is not lost in the group process.

• A program of high quality deserves support services of equally high quality. As the entree is the centerpiece of a banquet, instruction is the centerpiece of education. But neither entree nor instruction can stand alone; quality support and service are required in both cases. Professionalism in every aspect of planning is required. Educators preside over program design, and social planners orchestrate the logistical details of food and entertainment events. This symbiotic relationship is the very essence of the learning sanctuary.

Roger E. Comley is associate director for hotel and operating services, Georgia Center for Continuing Education, University of Georgia. He has also served as general manager of a private hotel property.

Educational technology, if managed carefully, can bring realism, focused information, and individualized interaction into the learning sanctuary.

Technology in the Learning Sanctuary

Robert L. Williams

Adult learning facilities—be they formal or informal, public or private— offer adults a place to learn away from the distractions of work, family, and community. However, without a sense of just those realities from which the learner has been separated, adult learning never leads to changes in behavior, job productivity, or social attitudes. This chapter examines ways in which educational technology can introduce a sense of reality into the learning sanctuary.

Mechanical Monsters in the Garden

The very notion of sanctuary as a place separated from the world suggests, at least in the modern world, a place separated from the intrusions of technology. The image of technology that comes to many minds is of mechanical monsters, Frankensteinian in their clumsy and naively evil ways, interrupting the otherwise highly humanistic and profoundly engaging spirit of the residential conference facility. I have another image in mind, however. As a child I lived in Japan. I once entered the interior garden of a traditional Japanese family home. By any description it was aesthetically and spiritually a sanctuary. The patriarch of the family, a papa-*san* in his eighties, sat on a stone bench in the afternoon sun by a pool, an open book on his lap. The book, his son explained, contained the Kanji characters of haiku, or short, unrhymed verse. The formal symmetry of the garden, with only a few specimen plants, allowed the mind to empty, said the son. The poems filled it back up again. The learning sanctuary can be seen as that garden, educational technology as that book.

Educational Technology and Reality in Learning. The modern conference center depends on educational media to focus, engage, inform, evaluate, and project many different views of the world for learners and thinkers. In the broadest sense, educational technology can be defined as a system for designing, developing, using, and evaluating teaching and learning. Educational technology coordinates people and instructional media "to promote more effective learning and gain increasing precision in control of environmental factors involved in learning" (Gillett, 1973, p. 2). Educational technology can be defined as anything—book, videotape, person, or three-dimensional object—that is a carrier of information. Thus, educational technologies "convey information, affect the message conveyed, control what is learned, and help establish the learning environment. They interact with the learner, helping determine what he or she sees and his or her attitude toward the world" (Gillett, 1973, p. 3).

Educational technology presents types of reality through different media (Allen, 1967; Briggs, 1972; Dale, 1969; and Wager, 1982). At one end of the continuum are media that are heavily dependent on symbols, both verbal and visual, and that give little concrete representation of reality. One example would be a college calculus textbook. At the other end of the continuum are media that are highly representational of reality and that use concrete forms. A three-dimensional simulation of the cockpit of an airplane with real-time stimulus and response would be one example.

How much reality does educational technology need to represent to be effective? The current wisdom suggests that we need a range between the poles of symbolic abstraction and direct representation (Wager, 1982). To improve information transfer, also, some combination of both affective (or attitude change) and cognitive (or knowledge transfer) mechanisms appears to be necessary. There is also an efficiency value operating along the continuum. The more abstract and symbolic media tend to compress the transfer of more material into less time. However, the more representational side of the continuum seems to replicate contextual or cultural settings, which improve retention and later application of learning (Pea, 1988).

Most theories of adult learning suggest that information transfer can be vastly improved by allowing the learner to place new information in both the format and context of previous and anticipated experiences. Studies suggest that there will be a higher rate of information transfer if the learner finds common elements—rather than common concepts—in both the learning and the application situations (Pea, 1988). It appears that successful transfers involve more than just memory or rote learning. For example, students are more likely to use math principles when shopping than for solving "invented" problems in the classroom. If the educator can connect new learning to a real-life context, then the student retains more new information and applies it in real life.

The problem with a learning sanctuary, which separates students from their normal reality, is that it diminishes the impact of three major factors important to the transfer and application of knowledge. First, it removes the learners from their daily context. The learner associates new information with books and classrooms, not with a daily job. Second, it reduces the factors that effectively mediate information transfer. The learner is removed from the modeling behavior of peers and the support of a workplace or community mentor. Third, it reduces the perceived function of new information or concepts. The learner learns better when work or social settings immediately reinforce or give value to new knowledge. Educators can overcome, at least in part, the absence of "reality" in most adult learning settings by using instructional representations that have both natural-appearing sequences and natural variability so that learners see "family resemblances" with their normal experiences, useful in later transfer settings (Pea, 1988, pp. 187–188). In other words, educational technology that presents obvious, and repetitive, patterns in problem-solving situations will result in learning that has little effect in the highly variable settings of reality.

Economics of Educational Technology. Aesthetics and learning theory aside, the argument for a place for educational technology in the learning sanctuary can be made on economics alone. Traditional funding strategies for residential or corporate learning facilities for adults are most typically figured on a "cost-per-unit" basis. As long as learning activities follow the group-conference model for teaching and learning, the cost per unit remains low and can be recovered. However, the needs of adult learners seem to contradict the methods of group learning (Knowles, 1978; Knox, 1977). If the residential facility pursues more individualized learning methods, then the cost per unit increases, often beyond any expectations for recovery.

Educational technology offers many attributes that can reduce the cost of individualized instruction. Because most modern educational technology is mechanically efficient (that is, uses small amounts of input to accomplish teaching and learning functions), it can reduce the cost per unit of highly individualized repetitive methods. Second, because most modern educational technology is computer-based, it has the potential for highly interactive and individualized instruction. Unfortunately, it is not the financial panacea many had forecast. Educational technology that sits idle through 50 to 60 percent of the first five years of ownership has little hope of recovering its investment before becoming obsolete (Wagner, 1982).

Contributions of Educational Technology

Clearly, the discussion so far presents a poor apology for the presence of "mechanical monsters" in the sanctuary. To many adult educators, educational technology remains as tempting as the apple in the Garden of Eden, and the consequences as dire. These attitudes will not be changed by information alone. The remaining sections of this chapter will explore fundamental contributions that educational technology can nevertheless make in creating a learning sanctuary within a conference center. Personal experiences with three very different adult residential learning facilities are used to illustrate the three fundamental contributions of educational technology, discussed shortly. The three facilities are described below.

1. The Highlander Research and Education Center in New Market, Tennessee, was founded by Myles Horton in 1932 after the model of the Danish folk school. The center has served as a residential learning facility for groups as diverse as an Appalachian women's economic cooperative, labor unions, environmental groups, and the National Association for the Advancement of Colored People.

2. The National Institute for Corrections, Boulder, Colorado, is the largest residential training facility for federal, state, and local prison employees. Financed in part by the federal government, the institute focuses on both the hard skills of maintaining a correctional facility and the soft skills of inmate development and rehabilitation.

3. The Georgia Center for Continuing Education, one of the nation's largest residential facilities on a university campus, opened in 1957. As part of the University of Georgia, the Georgia Center plays a significant role in the public service mission of a major land-grant university.

Each of these facilities seeks to create a learning sanctuary for widely different types of learners and each of them focuses on educational technology as diverse as community-based video production, computer-assisted open learning, and full environmental simulations. Diversity of technology used notwithstanding, all three of the facilities display common characteristics in the way educational technology enhances the learning-sanctuary concept. The three common contributions of educational technology to the learning sanctuary discussed in more detail in the following sections are: (1) technology's ability to focus and distill information, (2) its ability to introduce controlled representations of external reality, and (3) its ability to provide truly individualized learning.

Media Enhancement: Focusing and Distilling Information. The first major contribution educational technology can make to the learning sanctuary is by creating learning icons that help the learner put together different pieces of information. These learning icons can be distributed within the learning sanctuary much as statuary is distributed in a garden or religious images in a convent. An example of a learning icon is a poster hung in a conference setting that reminds the learner of the conference's purpose or of real-world issues the conference addresses. In the original Greek (*eikon*), icon meant not just any image or figure but a sacred image or figure. The word has come to hold a special meaning for representations that do more than replicate, or stand for, just one idea or concept. Icons typically represent sets of concepts that are interrelated.

Educational technology can enhance either the presentation of information or the information itself in one of six ways (Rosenthal, 1971). First, media produces intentional content-related effects. A videotape can show people the correct way to assemble mechanical parts, and people can then stop the tape and replicate the actions in real life. Second, media produces intended structural and compositional effects of the material. For instance, management training videotapes that use women in positive management roles may alter the viewer's concept of gender and management. Third, media affects how we view causal and interpersonal relationships. Fiction films and television series often give dramatic revelations of social conditions (*The Grapes of Wrath*) or mask social problems (*Leave It to Beaver*).

Fourth, media communicates a wide range of values, both about the way the world should operate and the way the world might operate. In particular, training videos based on case studies may imply a concept that the world is fair and just (hard work leads to promotions or salary raises) or that the world is not (hard work leads to stress and burnout). Fifth, media may contain unintended and contrary or contradictory effects unseen by media designers or altered by changing conditions. A 1950s documentary film called *Reefer Madness*, which had originally been produced to discourage the use of marijuana (primarily through overly dramatized case studies and misleading medical information), enjoyed a popular revival in the 1960s as a comedy film among American youth.

Sixth, media produces certain second-order effects that are both unintended and unanticipated but have a dramatic effect on unrelated audiences or ideas. The U.S. Armed Forces encouraged widespread media coverage of the war in Vietnam, including sending "media helicopters" daily to battlefields, in hopes of increasing military funding and support. Instead, the dramatic footage of soldiers in battle galvanized a generation of students (many of whom were draftable) to oppose the war.

Media effects, therefore, can be viewed as creating a composite icon that focuses and distills information. The electronic impulses on videotape or black type against white paper create recognizable images or symbols that transfer information. However, the potential for media enhancement (that is, the composite of media effects) creates relationships between images, and those relationships also suggest meanings. The numeral 2 or the letters c-a-t, by themselves, transfer information. The use of a story in which a black cat walks under a ladder combines two images and suggests superstition or bad luck.

One example of an adult learning facility that uses media icons to focus and distill information is the Highlander Center. Since its inception, Highlander has valued a residential learning experience that is group centered. The educational technology remained very simple for years: rocking chairs, stories, and songs. Even though the process was backed by technical information and an occasional outside expert, founder Myles Horton focused on the resources of the community in which he was working. Information was gathered through *participatory action research* and shared in stories or songs that were rich in common icons. In recent years, however, the Highlander Center has found that videotapes, produced in the community by community members and then shared at the center in programs dealing with environmental issues, enhanced the simple stories used with detailed icons of environmental problems.

For years, the local residents of a small, undeveloped "cove" or valley in the Appalachian Mountains of eastern Tennessee had been concerned about the dumping of unmarked metal drums in a private landfill. Through research and legal action, they finally forced the closing of the landfill. The residents decided to document the moving of the barrels by state agencies. The resulting videotape shows, in mechanical repetition, one barrel after another torn from the ground by a hydraulic-powered backhoe and left to leak into a nearby river. The videotaped images of crushed barrels and leaking fluids became a powerful icon for learning and thinking about environmental issues at the center.

Media Control: Reflecting on Measured Reality. Learning sanctuaries teeter precipitously between contemplation and escapism. The modern adult learning facility likewise runs the risk of creating an environment so foreign to everyday life that the learner or thinker cannot connect new information to old problems. As mentioned earlier (Pea, 1988), information transfer can be improved simply by matching the *context for learning* with the *context for problem solving*.

The second contribution that educational technologies can make to the learning sanctuary is *to remove barriers of time and space and create a measured reality within the learning sanctuary*. What is "measured reality"? If an adult residential learning facility seeks to create a learning sanctuary, it must seek to limit the distractions of the everyday world, or to limit reality. On the other hand, without a contextual, real-life setting for learning, information transfer falters. What learning sanctuaries need, therefore, are small doses of reality, carefully introduced at appropriate points in the learning experience and then neatly removed from view when they begin to distract. Measured realities can be defined as selected segments of reality captured at an earlier time through educational technology (videotape, audiotape, slides, three-dimensional simulations, and other techniques) and used to give a real-life context to a segment of learning or thinking.

The National Institute of Corrections provides a residential facility for federal, state, and local corrections officers near the campus of the University of Colorado, Boulder. The setting bears little resemblance to the prison facilities within which most of the learners work daily. After only a couple of years of operation, the institute found that some learners used their residential experience to reflect on professional issues and to seek out new techniques, but most of them reported a distinct drop in feelings of personal efficacy and application of new learning when they returned to the real world of prisons. Something, obviously, was not working. Therefore, rather than turn the facility into a retreat center, the program staff sought to interject pieces of reality into the learning setting.

Capitalizing on the ability to provide measured amounts of reality inherent in many educational technologies, the institute developed a series of videotapes and slide-tape presentations that mixed narrative stories of corrections officers on the job with learning goals. The series had well-developed characters (all of whom had both desirable and undesirable attitudes and behaviors), and each installment of the series had dramatic structure as well as technical content. More importantly, the series was well-researched by observing corrections officers on the job. It captured bits of reality in the settings, language, actions, and consequences depicted. This measured reality, then, could be introduced into the learning sanctuary to provide the context for information transfer.

The institute also developed a series of simulations of what the learners in residence would experience in their professional settings. The simulations ranged from full three-dimensional simulations to games that simulated the dynamics of the corrections system. The three-dimensional simulation consisted of cells and control rooms in a correctional facility into which predetermined problems (such as fire or a sick inmate) could be introduced. The learners played the roles of both corrections officers and inmates. The games, ostensibly designed for fun and relaxation but containing subtle messages, included a board game called "Walls" in which one group of players tried to construct a closed set of four walls around a mobile group of inmates. The actions on both sides were complicated by court decisions, local government, attorneys, escapes, and disasters. Another game, played out-of-doors, combined elements of blindman's bluff and rugby into "Jailball." The game tried to replicate the competitive dynamics between inmates and corrections officers.

Media Response: Interacting with the Individual. Educational historians disagree about which came first: linear learning or public education. Rather than debate theories of sequence surrounding America's contribution to the Industrial Age (the assembly line) and the advent of public education, there is abundant evidence that most of American education has a distinctly linear approach to learning. On the other hand, the concepts offered in this book lean toward a less linear and more self-directed approach in conference facilities. Unfortunately, espousing a philosophy of self-directed learning and practicing it are two different problems, for both the learner and the teacher. Every decision a teacher makes on the presentation of information and ideas begins to wear a path in the learning potential of that material. Learners are quick to pick up that path and pursue it to its ultimate conclusion, often without questioning.

The third contribution that educational technology can make to the learning sanctuary is to create highly individualized and interactive learning experiences that reduce the number of predetermined paths through them. Unfortunately, for readers who are thirty or older, this concept may be the most difficult to grasp. We are, in both our educational and entertainment experiences, products of linear learning.

Perhaps an example will help. Consider those of us born Pre-PacMan. We approach the screen of that early, popular video game and wiggle the knobs to the right, whereupon the video image goes to the right. We wiggle the knobs to the left, and the little chomping circle goes left. But what happened if the figure exited the top of the screen? Pre-PacMan would await the return of PacMan at the top of the screen. Post-PacMan (ten-year-olds who grew up on video games) knows to look immediately at the bottom of the screen. Video screens are not flat and linear but rather have a "video wrap." In the almost twenty years since the introduction of video games, there has been an explosion in the ability of computer-assisted educational technology to avoid the linear structure of its ancestors and to interact with the learner in ever widening circles of discovery.

Open learning systems are not only less likely to be linear, they are also less likely to display bias. Strange (1981) found that blacks and women report a preference for using computers because of a bias they often felt in white- and male-dominated settings. The term "open" refers to educational technology that can be entered from many different points (books tend not to make as much sense if you start reading on page 23), that allows the learner to move easily from section to section or level to level (graded textbooks purposefully avoid the use of words or concepts not "appropriate" to a given "level" of learning), and that can be reorganized by the learner (a videotape follows the same sequence no matter who is watching, whereas a well-designed videodisc could be watched twenty different ways in one afternoon).

The focus during the thirty-year history of the Georgia Center for Continuing Education has primarily been on group-centered learning experiences built around a conference, workshop, or seminar. However, over the past five years, with the support of the W. K. Kellogg Foundation, the center has begun an initiative to look at more individualized learning programs in an adult residential facility. One aspect of the individualized learning programs has been the application of educational technology; in particular, computer-assisted, nonlinear, highly interactive, or open-learning programs (Trott, 1987).

Open-learning programs exhibit an abundance of information that is graded or arranged by the program developer by (1) sequence, (2) complexity, and (3) location on the storage medium. That way, interactive programs can be written that *guide a learner through a sequence, introduce a learner to increasing levels of complexity,* or *allow the learner to select sections of information using some other organizing principle.* Even with the first two principles, the program developer builds in interactions with the learner that can be "evaluated" by the computer as a measure of the learner's preparedness to move on to the next sequence or level.

In particular, the Georgia Center found that *hypermedia* computer technology supported the nonlinear approach. Hypermedia is a generic term for a number of computer software families (like Apple's "HyperCard," Owl's "Guide," or IBM's "Linkway") that do not require advanced program skills but tie together large numbers of "stacks" of information. Hypermedia can be visualized as an extremely well-indexed set of books and slides. Think of being able to open a favorite book to an oft-quoted passage. Pick one word in that passage, "sanctuary," and touch it. When you do, it disappears and in its place are directions that let you find other mentions in the book of the word "sanctuary," a definition of "sanctuary," or pictures of sanctuaries in the other books and photos in your office. By connecting the computer to a laser videodisc (which, unlike the videotape, can be accessed quickly in a nonlinear fashion), the program developers have educational technology that is highly supportive of the individualized aspects of the learning sanctuary.

For instance, during a four-day-long conference on ethics in government, city managers follow an individualized residential learning program. Group meetings are limited to no more than two a day and are built around meals and a discussion format. The rest of the time, the city-manager-learners pursue individual learning activities including traditional readings and writing, plus individual "tutorials" with faculty in the School of Law, Department of Philosophy, and Institute of Government. The group also makes use of PALS (Personal Adult Learning Services), which offers videotapes on ethics and an original hypermedia program featuring cases of ethics in government.

Each city manager interacts with a computer-based case that includes sound, video, and text. By selecting key parts of the screen, including words in text or images within pictures, the learner moves himself or herself to new areas or levels of learning. Some areas are highly technical, others are more reflective; some areas lead the learner through predetermined sequences, in others the learner determines the relationships and order of events. The hypermedia program alone could engage a learner from fifteen minutes to over two hours, depending on the depth and breadth of information the learner selects.

Educational Technology in the Sanctuary

For those adult residential facilities that attempt to create a learning sanctuary, educational technology offers a cost-effective and flexible process by which (1) *to create information icons that allow the learner to focus on information*, (2) *to introduce measured bits of reality into the learning sanctuary*, and (3) *to develop open learning systems that are both interactive and nonlinear.* Educational technology, however, should not be viewed as an easy way to develop a learning sanctuary. An overabundance of educational technology can quickly turn education in a learning sanctuary into a passive experience in a dark room. Also, the high initial cost of most newer educational technologies precludes long-term experimentation with new media. Most institutions or organizations view their entry into sophisticated educational technology as an "all-or-nothing" plunge that requires the institution to speed up the acceptance process and begin using the new equipment quickly (Evans, 1982).

Educational technology has a significant role in the conference facility. However, the concept of sanctuary modifies the traditional role of educational technology in the classroom, either with children or with adults. The concept of sanctuary suggests the creation of a total, seamless environment for learning, living, and reflecting while in the residential facility. Educational technologies can contribute to the creation of that seamless environment only if educational media designers play an integral role in program development and in building the sanctuary, both in real and conceptual terms. Without such planning, the statues in the garden became mechanical monsters and the book of haiku, a chorus of jingles.

References

Allen, W. H. "Media Stimulus and Types of Learning." *Audio-Visual Instruction,* 1967, 2 (1), 27–31.

Briggs, L. J. *Students' Guide to Handbook of Procedures for the Design of Instruction.* Pittsburgh, Pa.: American Institute for Research, 1972.

Dale, E. *Audiovisual Methods in Teaching.* New York: Holt, Rinehart & Winston, 1969.

Evans, R. I. "Resistance to Innovations in Information Technology in Higher Education: A Social Psychological Perspective." In Sheehan, B. S. (ed.), *Information Technology: Innovations and Applications.* New Directions for Institutional Research, no. 35. San Francisco: Jossey-Bass, 1982.

Gillett, M. *Educational Technology: Toward Demystification.* Critical Issues in Canadian Education series. Scarborough, Ontario: Prentice-Hall of Canada, 1973.

Knowles, M. *The Adult Learner: A Neglected Species.* Houston, Tex.: Gulf Publishing, 1978.

Knox, A. B. *Adult Development and Learning: A Handbook on Individual Growth and Competence in the Adult Years.* San Francisco: Jossey-Bass, 1977.

Malone, T. W. "Toward a Theory of Intrinsically Motivating Instruction." *Cognitive Science,* 1981, 4, 333–369.

Pea, R. D. "Putting Knowledge to Use." In Nickerson, R. S., and Zodhiates, P. P. (eds.), *Technology in Education: Looking Toward 2020.* Hillsdale, N.J.: Erlbaum, 1988.

Rosenthal, R. A. "Media and Methodology in Effecting Change: Increasing Sense of Effectiveness Through Media." In L. Lipsitz (ed.), *Technology and Education: Articles from Educational Technology Magazine.* Englewood Cliffs, N.J.: Educational Technology Publications, 1971.

Strange, J. H. "Adapting to the Computer Revolution." In American Association of Higher Education (ed.), *New Technologies for Higher Education. Current Issues in Higher Education,* no. 5. Washington, D.C.: American Association of Higher Education, 1981.

Trott, A. J. (ed.). *Flexible Learning Systems. Aspects of Educational Technology,* vol. 20. London: Kogan Page, 1987.

Wager, W. *Instructional Technology and the Adult Learner.* Tallahassee, Fla.: International Institute of Andragogy, 1982.

Wagner, L. *The Economics of Educational Media.* New York: St. Martin's Press, 1982.

Robert L. Williams is associate director for communication services at the Georgia Center for Continuing Education and assistant professor in the College of Journalism and Mass Communications at the University of Georgia.

Success of the learning sanctuary depends on the careful selection
and training of personnel with a commitment to mission.

Human Resources for
the Learning Sanctuary

Jerry L. Hargis

This chapter will deal with human resources for the learning sanctuary. It
will also discuss elements of a desirable staffing structure and employee
philosophy. This structure and philosophy are often situational. That is,
each operation has come to its present form through a developmental
process that has blended history, tradition, politics, expediency, personalities, educational needs, and available resources. Nevertheless, discussing
basic principles of structure and objectives for staff selection, development,
and coordination can be useful. These basic concepts will be addressed as
the "Four Ps": philosophy, personnel, preparation, and presentation.

Philosophy

The philosophy that guides a residential conference center is also shaped
by history, personalities, and resources. But if the center is to be successful
in achieving the learning sanctuary ideal, it must concentrate on its product, which is the individual learning process provided through a short-
term learning experience that compacts the learning experience within an
efficiently used time frame.

For these short-term learning experiences to be successful on a continuing basis, it is necessary for each of the human resources in the center
to have a sense of "mission" and role. Staff should have an informed
commitment to maintaining a gestalt of human resource responses for
administrative, programmatic, and facilitative services. These responses
complement the "sanctuary" environment provided by the center. Where
the learning sanctuary may be the concept that describes the total environ-

ment of the center, mission is the concept that describes the soul of the center, which is the collective intent of its staff or human resources.

Key to the philosophical base of a center is defining its mission within the context of the learning sanctuary. When this is done, it is imperative that the mission be clearly articulated and available in writing. A center that has written its statement of mission has defined itself and can then begin to identify its human resource needs.

Personnel

In order for the learning sanctuary's educational programs to be successful, there must be an interface between the administrative, programmatic, and facilitative staff functions. For this interface to occur, there must be a knowledgeable staff with clear definitions of roles and responsibilities. Staff must perform their tasks with an attention to detail that leaves little to chance and that anticipates possible difficulties. This level of efficiency requires a commitment far above that of someone "just doing a job" and stresses a staff member's sense of mission. This commitment of staff can be illustrated with the following story. While taking a walk, a man comes upon a construction site. At the near end of the project he finds a worker laying bricks and asks, "What is it you are doing here?" The workman snaps back, "I'm laying bricks—what does it look like I'm doing?" The walker continues to the other end of the project, finds another worker similarly employed, and asks again, "What are you doing here?" With a smile the worker replies, "Sir, I am building a church." There is a considerable difference in attitude and understanding of mission between the worker just laying bricks and the worker who "has his eye on the steeple" by building a church.

The "steeple view" is the ability of the staff to look beyond the individual details of the learning activity and focus on overall educational objectives and desired outcomes for the various audiences served. Staff do this while working to enhance the accomplishments of the total program of educational access and presentation within the sanctuary.

Staff Functions. To be successful in the learning sanctuary, each of the three staff components (administration, program, and service) must understand this view and so coordinate their efforts that the resulting performance is all but invisible to the adult learners.

Administration. These staff members have tasks and responsibilities necessary for the maintenance of the conference center organization. Personnel in this area provide the infrastructure of the center. They serve to link the center administratively with the parent organization, maintain management functions, provide fiscal and administrative support services, and generally may be seen as the executive unit of the center.

Program. Depending on the nature of the center, there may or may not be educational programming staff. For example, institutions of higher education, corporate training centers, and religious centers have a central educational focus to their missions. Consequently, they require content specialists (faculty or consultants) as well as adult educators who design educational programs. Private sector conference centers, however, have central missions to provide outstanding physical facilities only to the external client. Thus, educational programming becomes the client's responsibility and programming staff are not retained in house by center management.

Services. Members of this staff provide support and enabling services for the physical and mechanical processes of the conference center. As in the other areas, there may be considerable overlap of personnel duties, depending on the size of the center. Service staff usually are identified as being "front of the house" or "back of the house," to distinguish between employees performing functions visible to conference participants and those who work behind the scenes. Staff jobs in the service areas include the hotel desk personnel, some food-service persons, cashiers, gift-shop attendants, and audio-visual specialists (all front of the house) and cooks, janitors, house and grounds-keeping crews, maintenance personnel, and copy-center operators (all back of the house).

Selection of Staff. Selecting staff may be among the most difficult of tasks, but there are four guidelines that can help. First, select the very best people available. This would appear to be an obvious strategy. Yet, managers often state that they wanted to hire someone but considered the individual "overqualified." In spite of the possibility that future job dissatisfaction might occur, never hesitate to hire an individual who may appear to be overqualified. Center leadership has the responsibility to provide sufficient challenge and responsibility to maintain the interest and commitment of employees. In all hiring situations look not just at the abilities that qualify an individual for the position (typing skills in a secretary, for example) but look also at what the individual can potentially provide the organization.

Second, where possible make each new hire an opportunity to reexamine existing staff work load and distribution. Conference centers often find themselves understaffed in areas with a heavy work load. New hires offer an opportunity to make necessary adjustments. New staff seldom have the skills, talents, or interests found in the employees they are replacing. Consequently, use new employees as an opportunity to realign tasks and relationships for improved organizational effectiveness.

Third, take ample time in the interview and selection process. Match assignments with the background and experience of the applicants. We often say that we must "grow our own" staff, and in some sense this is true because of the situationality in conference centers mentioned earlier. Use the interview and selection process as an opportunity to explain the learning-sanctuary concept and thus to begin the individual's orientation.

Fourth, when organizational circumstances permit, offer the possibility that an individual can "invent" her or his own job. The new staff member can define a combination of tasks and responsibilities that match closely personal interests and talents and, of course, organizational needs.

External Personnel Resources. Demands for service made on conference centers can exceed the capabilities of a center's own staff to respond. Thus, it becomes necessary to plan for the utilization of external human resources. The center mission statement helps identify the types of staff needed to provide audiences with an appropriate educational program. Private-sector conference centers generally leave responsibility for instructional design with the client. However, in an institution of higher education faculty are the central and, usually, most accessible human resource. In instances when faculty can be effectively informed of the service attitude and commitment to mission of center staff, many of them will "buy in" to the learning sanctuary concept. When this happens, the conference center has a real treasure of support and advocacy.

Where conference centers are not connected with higher education directly, center staff may deal with training directors, program designers, meeting planners, and others from the corporate world who must be viewed as clients, not staff. Additional external resources are the adult learners themselves and staff from other conference centers. This situation has advantages and disadvantages. Although external clients may be more demanding, at the same time, they have a vested interest in the success of the educational program and are highly motivated to make the relationship with the conference center successful.

Preparation

The next human resource issue that the learning sanctuary's management must address is staff orientation and training, or the third P, preparation. The central mission of any conference center is the starting point for staff development. If the central mission of the learning sanctuary is the development of external human resources, then conference center staff must also be included. Administrative and service-staff employees as well as program staff ideally should grasp the concept that theirs is a special place that exists for the educational development of adults. This central theme, when understood and committed to by the staff, will result in a gestalt that is the heart of the learning-sanctuary concept.

To understand this gestalt, it is important for staff to have an orientation program at the time of employment that clearly articulates the center's mission and values. Also, there must be on-going programs for staff development that reinforce that mission and individual responsibility in carrying out the objectives of the conference center. Only then can the staff of an adult learning center have a fair opportunity to understand and to internalize the spirit of the learning sanctuary.

In the late sixties, Bennis (1969) articulated an idea called "post-bureaucratic" leadership. He suggested that the modern organization would not consist of a pyramid style of leadership but instead would possess a style characterized by interlocking relationships of problem-solving teams composed of experts who came together around a specific issue. The teams would solve specific problems and then break up into other teams as conditions changed or new problems emerged.

The learning sanctuary works in a similar manner. In recent years at the University of Oklahoma's Center for Continuing Education, we have tried to use Bennis's model to develop a concept of shared leadership, full information flow, continuing statement and restatement of mission, clear definition of responsibilities and tasks, and (perhaps most difficult of all) a permissive administrative posture that allows staff, within reasonable limits, to get the job done in the way they think best. The essential point of this model is that staff training is focused on developing the entire person, including values and attitudes, not simply task definition and proficiency. When all staff are developed in this way—when development relates to the tasks *and* to the mission of the learning sanctuary—then chances of the individual staff member "buying in" as a stakeholder in the conference center's success are greatly increased.

Administration, program, and service-area staff, trained separately for task improvement, are educated together to achieve objectives in human development. Common-session formats also provide a mechanism to discuss mutual activities and problems as well as to get informal feedback from colleagues. Timely information on the characteristics of adult audiences visiting the conference center is provided so that center staff have an understanding of the client as an individual. The personalization of the various participant groups often leads to interaction between participants and staff that can lend a concerned, friendly, and supportive atmosphere of personal service to the learning sanctuary. Finally, center management has regular sessions for all staff on professional development topics in adult and continuing education. The understanding by everyone of the staff functions throughout a conference center assists in "cross training" and in building an informed perspective in staff members about the entire center and its mission.

The staff development program seeks to have the individual staff member view the achievement of the organization's mission to be in his or her best interest. When staff understand that they "work for people" and in so doing help develop individual human resources for more meaningful participation in a democratic society, they know that society as a whole has benefited from their work. Human resource development for the learning sanctuary must include necessary training for successful task performance. Further, it must explain the relationships of those tasks with other tasks, and, finally, it must provide inspiration and motivation for fulfilling the sanctuary's mission so that staff can work together for a common goal. When this is accomplished, staff are ready to support the short-term learning experiences provided by the residential conference center.

Presentation

Successful performance for a center results from successful presentation, the fourth P. The job of a conference center is, in a sense, to entertain. Consider the roots of the word *entertain,* from the Latin *intr* (between) and *tenere* (to hold). The function of "capturing" or "holding" the participant in an enriched learning environment is what the center is about. A bit of elegant showmanship is not a bad thing. When staff perform well, when facilities are professionally prepared and presented, when educational elements are outstanding, the result is masterly performance.

Here as elsewhere, people are the key. Professional-level performances from a cook or maid are every bit as important as the professionalism of the instructor. Professional excellence from each person in the center provides an experience for the participant that helps fulfill the learning-sanctuary concept.

Conclusion

In striving to have the best in human resources for the learning sanctuary:

- Hire the best people available
- Explain to them what they are to do
- Explain to them what a residential conference center does
- Relate their tasks to the center's mission
- Provide the resources necessary for the job
- Provide full information, training, and encouragement on a regular basis.

Staff are the key to the center's success. Well-defined statements of the learning sanctuary's mission, role, and process will greatly enhance the opportunity for success by individual staff members and thus by the center. The mission of the staff becomes an *informed* commitment to maintain a *gestalt* of human resource *responses* for administrative, programmatic, and facilitative services that complement the learning sanctuary. If we acknowledge the elements of "informed," "gestalt," and "response" in a truly cooperative effort, we will have staff who keep their eyes on the steeple.

Reference

Bennis, W. "Post-Bureaucratic Leadership." *Trans-action*, 1969, 6 (9), 44–53.

Jerry L. Hargis is assistant vice-provost for continuing education services at the University of Oklahoma. Among his responsibilities is management of the Oklahoma Center for Continuing Education.

The future of the residential conference center poses challenges for both researchers and practitioners.

Future Challenges for the Residential Conference Center

Carol E. Kasworm, Edward G. Simpson, Jr.

The chapters of this volume have addressed elements of the optimal residential adult educational center within the context of the learning-sanctuary concept. These elements include history, educational program, physical environment, atmosphere, technology, and human resources. The refinement and combination of these elements in just the right proportions create the learning sanctuary, that special educational retreat for the adult student. Yet, the difficulty in achieving this blend of ingredients requires from the conference-center profession (1) development and renewal of leadership, (2) skilled management practices, (3) on-going research into the nature of this approach to adult learning and, finally, (4) a vibrant and replenishing strategy for professional development. This chapter concludes our examination of the concept of the learning sanctuary by discussing these four requirements for the future health of the adult residential conference center movement and by providing a brief reflection on its current status.

Reflections

In contemporary society, residential conference centers have become highly valued contexts for mainstream adult-learning activities. Although vital examples of the traditions of the Danish folk school and residential school still exist, today's residential adult education presents an elaborate tapestry of variations on these original themes. Modern conference centers demonstrate a growing diversity in the public and private sectors. Today's centers reflect innovative architectural designs, unique geographic settings, increased entrepreneurial efforts, and more competitively designed strategic missions. Many of the newer conference centers feature both educational and technological support systems based on research and contemporary practice in adult learning. Additionally, residential centers face significant pressures for survival from escalating costs, a more competitive environment, and heightened expectations by adult learners concerning the quality of both the learning experience and the residential setting. In an age of diversity, choice, and quality, adult residential education faces many challenges.

For the future, effective leadership in residential adult education requires an appreciation and understanding of adult learning—both its past and its present. Of greater importance, leadership in the field is in need of a prototype, an image to guide and direct its future. The metaphor of the "learning sanctuary" presented in this volume can provide such an image.

Considerations in Planning for the Future

The evolutionary process affecting residential conference centers, as described by Buskey in Chapter Two, seems certain to continue. Thus, today's conference professional, as well as the adult-education researcher, must prepare for a future where the only constant for the field is that of change. Consequently, practitioner and theorist must discover or create new paradigms for leadership, management, research, and renewal.

Leadership. Although many adult education practitioners have fostered residential education, the field's professional organizations have been relatively silent about planning for and bringing about growth and diversification. Even the literature lags somewhat. Leadership is needed that creates and communicates innovations in residential adult education. All those connected with the field—providers, practitioners, and researchers—are encouraged to reflect on, discuss, and research the salient issues affecting residential adult education. Sharing successes and failures and exchanging ideas can help develop a network of conference center professionals, particularly of those in higher education.

A few groups already address issues related to conference centers and residential education. As noted in Chapter Two, the W. K. Kellogg Foundation has played a major role in the development of adult residential conferencing for higher education. Through both regular meetings and specialty conferences, the Kellogg family of conference centers (located at nine universities in this country and at one in England) wrestle with the issues raised in this volume and seek to build a productive future. Other universities, as well as the National University Continuing Education Association (NUCEA), hold meetings about various aspects of the conference center business and the development of quality residential education. The International Association of Conference Centers (IACC) offers yet another mechanism for involved professionals (particularly from the private sector) to discuss and reflect on the nature of this enterprise.

There remains, however, a growing need for increased discussion and collaborative exchange among conference center professionals. Meeting this need can be accomplished in several ways. For example, the professional associations in adult and continuing education should actively provide leadership in this effort. A sub-unit, a task force, or a specialty group could be formed (in some cases rejuvenated) in an association to study, analyze, and exchange innovative practices and planning models related to conference centers. Whatever the mechanism, it is a propitious time to bring together groups in higher education and the private sector. To meet future challenges, professional unity is required.

Management Practices. Residential conference center operators of today must emphasize sound management practices. Increasingly, conference center professionals in higher education feel the pressure to generate revenue and to improve their managerial efficiency (this has always been true in the private sector). This pressure can be attributed to the competitive and unpredictable business environment and the need to have an operation that produces a surplus, just like any other successful business. Adding to these pressures are adult learners who expect and insist on an increasingly higher standard of quality. Further, dedicated conference facilities require significant up-front capital investment, long-term debt retirement, and a never-ending chain of capital replacement projects. Consequently, effective management and financial accountability are major elements in survival and success.

In short, it is costly to operate a residential conference center. We have seen how some institutions join with the private sector in joint ventures in order to help minimize liabilities and the need for specialized management expertise. The institution coordinates and plans the educational program while private firms (hotels, restaurants, even university residence-hall facilities, in some cases) provide housing and food services. While these joint ventures may yield some fiscal or management benefits for both the institutional conference center and the external party, this divided arrangement restricts development of the relationship between the residential living environment and the adult-learning experience. Consequently, the "learning sanctuary" suffers.

With joint ventures, adult educators cannot regulate or influence the design and operation of the complete living and learning environment. Unlike stoic adult learners in years past, adults today are hesitant to stay in a dormitory facility with community showers and poor amenities. Sparse accommodations often negatively influence the psychological comfort of adult learners. Conversely, adults who are housed in opulent resort like facilities may encounter difficulty remaining focused on the educational objective; they may succumb to recreational distractions. The challenge for organizations using joint ventures is to develop an effective balance between the educational experience offered by the learning sanctuary and the enrichment created by its support facilities.

Research. There has been limited research and writing on residential adult education during the last twenty years, a fact that Buskey dramatically underscores in Chapter Nine with his bibliographical analysis. This lack of documented discussion of current practice, of conceptual models, and of a research agenda is very disheartening. A conference center dedicated to residential adult education represents one of the most useful educational environments for systematic research on adult learning, on program designs, on the influences of environment on learning, and on adult-learner development. With so many subjects available, we encourage more study, research, and exchanges between adult educators from both higher education and the business sectors.

Professional Development. As professionals in an evolving field, practitioners of residential adult education have primarily gained expertise through problem-solving, research, reflection, and collaboration with colleagues. We encourage practitioners to work with adult education graduate programs in preparing the next generation of professionals. For example, a renewed effort to combine courses in adult learning, program design, and business management with specific internships in residential centers should provide valuable experiences for prospective practitioners not only in adult education graduate programs but also in schools of hotel and restaurant management as well. Additionally, professional development seminars and graduate courses concerning effective residential adult education and conference center management are needed. Also, leading adult education centers and residential facilities should experiment with new and innovative practices; risk-taking should be an important element in an effective learning sanctuary.

Conclusion

Practitioners have the responsibility to examine continually their methods of operation, as well as to reflect on the reasons they conduct their practice as they do. Conversely, the adult education researcher who reflects on the theoretical and historical foundations for certain practices needs to be ever mindful of the pragmatism so characteristic of the workplace and its environment of applied research. Both perspectives are essential to a healthy conference center organization.

In conclusion, the learning sanctuary of the future will serve an increasingly sophisticated and knowledgeable clientele. The professionals working in residential conference centers who construct a philosophical foundation based on the rich history and tradition of adult residential learning, and who then pause to reflect and to question the paradigm of the learning sanctuary, will improve, strengthen, and renew this unique educational experience.

Carol E. Kasworm is associate professor of adult education at the University of Tennessee, Knoxville.

Edward G. Simpson, Jr., is director of the Georgia Center for Continuing Education and associate professor of adult education at the University of Georgia.

The following list of resources on the operation, philosophy, and history of conference centers and residential adult education should help stimulate the writing in the field.

Bibliography of the Literature on Conference Centers and Residential Adult Education

John H. Buskey

Literature represents the knowledge base of a field of practice and can be a rich source of ideas, information, and inspiration. This bibliography is intended to be a comprehensive, though not exhaustive, compilation of the literature on conference centers and residential adult education. It is presented here in the hope that it will stimulate and encourage present-day practitioners and students of residential adult education to investigate the philosophical, historical, and operational beginnings of such education and to acquaint themselves with Grundtvig, Houle, Livingstone, Schacht, and the many others who have written about the residential education concept and its values in developing programs for adults.

A Commentary on the Documents in the Bibliography

The bibliography contains 194 documents on practice, theory, philosophy, history, facilities, programs, and operations of conference centers and residential adult education programs. When the bibliography was completed, data on publication dates, types of documents, and country of publication were compiled in order to identify any trends that might be helpful to researchers and practitioners. Space limitations did not permit the inclusion of the complete analysis. For further information the reader should contact the author of this chapter. The total number of publications in the bibliography (194) is not very large when one considers the substantial amount of money that has been invested in residential conference

NEW DIRECTIONS FOR ADULT AND CONTINUING EDUCATION, no. 46, Summer 1990 © Jossey-Bass Inc., Publishers centers in the last fifty years and the even larger investment in programs that have been conducted in the centers. Further, the annual output appears to be declining as illustrated in Figure 1, which shows the number of documents in the bibliography by year of publication, in five-year increments except for the first.

As shown in Figure 1, only 31.4 percent of the documents have been published in the last fifteen years, while 27.7 percent were published in the five-year period 1965–1969; in the 1965–1971 seven-year period, seventy-seven documents (39.7 percent of the total) were published. This was a period of time when several of the Kellogg-supported centers had just been established and funds had simultaneously been provided to a few universities for graduate study and research in residential adult education. Clearly there has been an increase in the conference center movement: There are many new university and private centers, there are more programs, there are more staff, there has been considerable commercial interest, and the list goes on. What is curious and difficult to understand is that parallel with this activity has been a substantial reduction in scholarly production, and even popular writing about the topic is modest. Despite the larger number of centers in existence, residential adult education apparently has declined as an area of interest for researchers and writers.

Conventions Used in the Bibliography

In the bibliography presented below, items that appear in the ERIC data base are marked with an asterisk (*) at the end of each citation, those in the Dissertation Abstracts International data base are marked with a pound

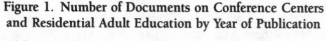

Figure 1. Number of Documents on Conference Centers and Residential Adult Education by Year of Publication

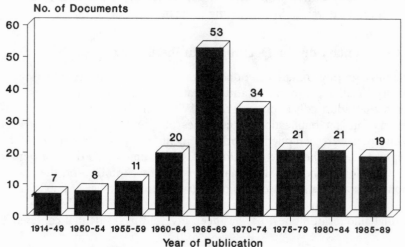

sign (#) at the end of each citation, and bibliographies are noted with (BIB) at the end of the citation. Documents available in microfiche or hard copy from the ERIC Document Reproduction Service (EDRS) are labeled with the ED number at the end of the citation. The total number of pages in each document, when known, is given at the end of the citation.

Bibliography

Adams, F. *Unearthing Seeds of Fire: The Idea of Highlander.* Winston-Salem, N.C.: Blair, 1975.

Aker, George F. *Adult Education Procedures, Methods and Techniques: A Classified and Annotated Bibliography, 1953–1963.* Syracuse, N.Y.: Library of Continuing Education and University College, Syracuse University, 1965, 163 pp. (BIB)

Alford, Harold J. "A History of Residential Adult Education." Unpublished doctoral dissertation, Department of Education, University of Chicago, 1966, 442 pp. * #

Alford, Harold J. *Continuing Education in Action: Residential Centers for Lifelong Learning.* New York: Wiley, 1968, 162 pp. *

Alford, Harold J. *The Evolution of an Idea: From Danish Folk High School to Residential Center for Continuing Education.* Continuing Education Report, no. 18. Chicago: University of Chicago, 1969, 4 pp.

Altenbaugh, Richard J., and Paulston, Rolland G. "Work People's College: A Finnish Folk High School in the American Labor College Movement." *Paedagogica Historica,* 1978, *18,* 237–256.

Ames, Kenneth L. "The Winterthur Museum as Conference Center." *Continuum,* 1984, *48* (2), 130–136.

Ashmore, Owen, and Smith, Derek. "University Residential Adult Education." *Adult Education (British),* 1982, *54* (4), 336–341. *

Axford, Roger W. *Adult Education: The Open Door.* Scranton, Pa.: International Textbook, 1969, 247 pp. *

Barnett, Chris. "Great Office Escapes." *Mainliner* (United Airlines), Oct. 1975, 37–39.

Begtrup, Holger; Lund, Hans; and Manniche, Peter. *The Folk High Schools of Denmark and the Development of a Farming Community.* London: Oxford University Press, 1949.

Bell, Norris H. "Self-Sufficiency: Can Centers for Continuing Education Be Self-Supporting?" Proceedings of Kansas State University Conference on "The Role of Non-Credit Programs in Higher Education: Administrative Issues." Denver, Colo., June 20–22, 1982, 37–42.

Bell, Norris H. "The Velvet Rack: The Value of Having the Conference Center Closely Tied to the University Organizational Structure." *Continuum,* 1984, *48* (2), 137–139.

Bland, Laurel L. "A Center for Continuing Education in Alaska: Innovation for a Developing Area." 1970, 15 pp. (ED 037 655) *

Boyer, Lester L. "Impact of Visual Cues on Speech Perception in Conference Centers." Unpublished doctoral dissertation, University of California, Berkeley, 1976, 161 pp. #

Bradtke, Joel H. "Successful Meetings: A Practical Application. The National Conference Center's Approach." *Training and Development Journal*, 1974, 28 (1), 3–7. *

Brown, Andrew M. "The Organization and Administration of a New Residential College." *Adult Education (British)*, 1950, 23 (2), 122–127.

Brown, W. Rex. "A Report of Selected Residential Continuing Education Centers in the United States." Orlando, Fla.: University of Central Florida, 1980, 108 pp. (ED 221 075) *

Buskey, John H. "The Development and Testing of a Typology of Adult Education Programs in University Residential Centers." Abstract of doctoral dissertation, University of Chicago, 1970, 29 pp. (ED 041 235) *

Buskey, John H. "The Development and Testing of a Typology of Adult Education Programs in University Residential Centers." Unpublished doctoral dissertation, University of Chicago, 1970, 284 pp.

Buskey, John H. "Residential Conference Centers: The Past, the Present and the Future." *Continuum*, 1984, 48 (1), 1–11. *

Campbell, Olive Dame. *The Danish Folk School.* New York: Macmillan, 1928.

Canadian Association for Adult Education. *Residential Adult Education Centres in Canada: A Directory.* Toronto, Ontario: Canadian Association for Adult Education, 1966, 20 pp. (ED 011 982) *

Canadian Institute for Adult Education. *Les Centres Residentiels* [Residential Centers]. Montreal, Quebec: Canadian Institute for Adult Education, 1968, 73 pp. (ED 026 586) *

Capes, Mary (ed.). *Communication or Conflict. Conferences: Their Nature, Dynamics, and Planning.* New York: Association Press, 1960, 228 pp.

"A Center for Conferences and Continuing Education." Philadelphia: University City Science Center, 1966, 42 pp. (ED 019 833) *

Civil Service Commission. "Off-Campus Study Centers for Government Employees." Pamphlet T-4, rev. ed. Washington, D.C.: U.S. Government Printing Office, 1971, 163 pp. (ED 053 361) *

Cobb, Alice. "Residential Workshops: The Case for Them." *Adult Leadership*, 1961, 9 (9), 278–281.

Cody, Dan. "Unconventional Conventions." *Sky* (Delta Airlines), Feb. 1980, pp. 63–64, 66–67.

Coleman, David S. "A Study of the Leader Behavior of Selected Directors of University Conference Operations." Unpublished doctoral dissertation, University of Wisconsin, 1969, 152 pp.

Collins, Michael. "Quality Learning Through Residential Conferences." In P. J. Ilsley (ed.), *Improving Conference Design and Outcomes.* New Directions for Continuing Education, no. 28. San Francisco: Jossey-Bass, 1985, 69–75. *

"Conference Center Serves as a Solar Lab." *American School and University*, 1977, 49 (6), 22–23, 25. *

Craig, Wayne O. "A Reaction to John Buskey." *Continuum*, 1984, *48* (2), 143-145.

Crane, Carlson E. "A Critical Analysis of Selected University Continuing Education Centers in the United States." Unpublished Ed.D. dissertation, New York University, 1959, 238 pp. #

Cross, Wilbur. *The Weekend Education Source Book.* New York: Harper's Magazine Press, 1976, 296 pp.

Curtis, Joan C. "The Effects of a Physical Activity on Learner Satisfaction During a Conference (Exercise)." Unpublished Ed.D. dissertation, University of Georgia, 1985, 98 pp. #

Davies, Joss. "Some Notes on Residential Adult Education." *Australian Journal of Adult Education*, 1972, *12* (2), 61-66. *

Davis, David C. L. "The Danish Folk Highschool: An Experiment in Humanistic Education." Unpublished doctoral dissertation, United States International University, 1969, 179 pp.

Davis, David C. L. *Model for a Humanistic Education: The Danish Folk Highschool.* Columbus, Ohio: C. E. Merrill, 1971, 132 pp.

Day, Harry P. "The New England Center for Continuing Education: A Consortium of Six States." *Journal of the International Congress of University Adult Education (Canada)*, 1970, *9* (3), 13-16. *

Day, Harry P. "Switch ON for Continuing Education." *International Journal of Continuing Education and Training*, 1973, *3* (2), 93-97. *

Dekker, Tunis H. *Is University Faculty Committed to Conference Programs?* Continuing Education Report, no. 13. Chicago: University of Chicago, 1967, 5 pp.

Densmore, Max L. "An Evaluative Analysis of Selected University Conference Programs Conducted at Kellogg Center for Continuing Education, Michigan State University." Unpublished doctoral dissertation, Michigan State University, 1965, 191 pp. * #

Deppe, Donald A. "The Conference Director as a Boundary Definer of the University." Unpublished doctoral dissertation, Department of Education, University of Chicago, 1965.

Deppe, Donald A. *The Director of Conference Programming: His Attitudes Toward Job Role.* Continuing Education Report, no. 6. Chicago: University of Chicago, 1965, 4 pp.

Deppe, Donald A. "The Adult Educator: Marginal Man and Boundary Definer." *Adult Leadership*, 1969, *18* (4), 119-120, 129-130.

Devlin, Laurence E., and Litchfield, Ann. *Residential Program Data—A Statistical Description.* Continuing Education Report, no. 15. Chicago: University of Chicago, 1967, 6 pp. *

Devlin, Laurence E., and Litchfield, Ann. *Residential Program Data—Implications for Practice.* Continuing Education Report, no. 16. Chicago: University of Chicago, 1967, 6 pp. *

Diekhoff, John S. "Residential Education: No Place Like Home." *Adult Education*, 1960, *10* (4), 238-246.

A Directory of Residential Continuing Education Centers in the United States, Canada, and Abroad, 1967–68. Chicago: Studies and Training in Continuing Education, University of Chicago, 1968, 156 pp. (ED 027 497) *

Dolce, Andy. "University-Based Conference Centers: Extending the Educational Process." American School and University, 1978, 51 (1), 65–66. *

Doyle, Louis A. A Developing Continuing Education Centre in Nsukka, Nigeria. Continuing Education Report, no. 10. Chicago: University of Chicago, 1966, 4 pp.

Doyle, Louis A. "Continuing Education—Nsukka: A Program of University Extension Aimed at Serving the Practical and Intellectual Needs of a Developing Nation." 1969, 66 pp. (ED 026 577) *

Draves, William A. "Analyzing Trends in Conference Design." In P. J. Ilsley (ed.), Improving Conference Design and Outcomes. New Directions for Continuing Education, no. 28. San Francisco: Jossey-Bass, 1985.

Duberman, Martin. Black Mountain; An Exploration in Community. New York: Dutton, 1972, 527 pp.

Duke, C. "Universities in the Community—The Role of the CCE's and Extension Services." Journal of Tertiary Educational Administration (Australia), 1980, 2 (1), 51–61. *

Durston, Berry H. "Some Characteristics of Participants in Residential Adult Education." Australian Journal of Adult Education, 1970, 10 (1), 17–19. *

"Education Center Reflects Adult Perspectives." College and University Business, 1970, 49 (5), 57–59. *

Education for Life. Proceedings of the International Conference on the Occasion of the Bicentenary of N.F.S. Grundtvig. Copenhagen: Det Danske Selskab, 1983.

Eklund, Lowell R., and McNeil, Donald R. The University and Residential Education. The University and Continuing Education. University Extension Bulletin, no. 8. New Brunswick, N.J.: University Extension Division, Rutgers–The State University, 1970, 25 pp. (ED 049 405) *

Fales, Ann Wohlleben. The Pattern of Anxiety in Residential Conferences. Continuing Education Report, no. 11. Chicago: University of Chicago, 1966, 6 pp.

Fishelman, Arthur. "You Owe It to Your Trainees to Try the Total Learning Environment of a Conference Center." Training, 1978, 15 (5), 43–44. *

Fleck, Sir Alexander; Stephens, Leslie; Maclennan, A.; and Cherrington, Paul. "Residence and Technical Education." Adult Education [British], 1960, 33 (1), 6–12.

Florell, Robert J. "Applicational Transfer in Adult Education." Unpublished doctoral dissertation, Department of Adult Education, University of Nebraska, 1966, 454 pp.

Foght, H. W. The Danish Folk High Schools. Washington, D.C.: U.S. Government Printing Office, 1914.

Ford, James H. "A Critical Study of the Continuing Adult Student Body at the Oklahoma Center for Continuing Education in Programs of Liberal Education." Unpublished doctoral dissertation, University of Oklahoma, 1966, 102 pp. * #

Franklin, Richard. "Effective Workshops in Human Relations." *Journal of Educational Sociology,* 1955, *28* (9), 381-388.

Fraser, W. R. *Residential Education.* Oxford, England: Pergamon Press, 1968, 312 pp.

Friend, L. L. *The Folk High Schools of Denmark.* Washington, D.C.: U.S. Government Printing Office, 1914.

Fuller, Jack W. "Building for Adult Education." *International Journal of Career and Continuing Education,* 1975, *1* (1), 25-33. *

Gage, Gene G. "The Nordic Example." *Saturday Review,* 1975, *3* (26), 19-21.

Goebel, Edward L. "An Analysis of Related Organizational Patterns in University Adult Education Centers and Their Parent Institutions: A Study in Dual Hierarchy." Unpublished doctoral dissertation, University of Georgia, 1969.

Gould, Joseph E. *The Chautauqua Movement: An Episode in the Continuing American Revolution.* Albany, N.Y.: State University of New York Press, 1961.

Grabowski, Stanley M. "Residential Adult Education." *Adult Leadership,* 1971, *19* (10), 356. * (BIB)

Grozier, Gillian. "The World of Chautauqua." *Piedmont* (USAir), 1989, *11* (6), 24-28.

Grundtvig, N.F.S. *Selected Writings: N.F.S. Grundtvig.* (J. Knudsen, ed. and trans.) Philadelphia: Fortress, 1976.

Grundtvig, N.F.S., and Alford, Harold J. *The School for Life.* Continuing Education Report, no. 5. Chicago: University of Chicago, 1965, 4 pp.

Gunn, Bill L. "The Developing Role of the Georgia Center for Continuing Education in Local Community Problem-Solving." Unpublished dissertation, Department of Education, University of Georgia, 1973, 167 pp. #

Harris-Worthington, Phillip. "Back to the Future: A Study of Short-Term Adult Residential Education." Paper presented at the Annual Conference of Principals of Short-Term Adult Residential Colleges, Devizes, Wiltshire, England, May 1987, 45 pp. (ED 297 135) *

Hart, Joseph K. *Light from the North: The Danish Folk High Schools and Their Meaning for America.* New York: Holt, Rinehart & Winston, 1927.

Hoiberg, Otto G. "The Saugeen Seminar." *Adult Leadership,* 1961, *9* (8), 243-244, 255.

Holt, Robert N. "A Study of the Background and Functions of Selected Directors of University Operated Residential Centers for Continuing Education." Unpublished master's thesis, Virginia Polytechnic Institute and State University, 1978, 70 pp.

Horton, Aimee. "The Highlander Folk School, Pioneer of Integration in the South." *Teachers College Record,* 1966, *68* (3), 242-250.

Houle, Cyril O. *The Training Function of the Center for Continuing Education.* Continuing Education Report, no. 8. Chicago: University of Chicago, 1965, 4 pp.

Houle, Cyril O. *University-Level Continuing Education.* Continuing Education Report, no. 7. Chicago: University of Chicago, 1965, 4 pp.

Houle, Cyril O. *What Is Continuing Education?* Continuing Education Report, no. 1. Chicago: University of Chicago, 1965, 4 pp.

Houle, Cyril O. *The Research Function of the Center for Continuing Education.* Continuing Education Report, no. 9. Chicago: University of Chicago, 1966, 4 pp.

Houle, Cyril O. *Residential Continuing Education.* Notes and Essays on Education for Adults, no. 70. Syracuse, N.Y.: Syracuse University Publications in Continuing Education, 1971, 86 pp.

Hunter, Guy. "Short-Term Residential Colleges—Towards a Definition." *Adult Education* [British], 1951, 23 (4), 285–289.

Hunter, Guy. *Residential Colleges: Some New Developments in British Adult Education.* Occasional Papers, no. 1. New York: Fund for Adult Education, 1952.

International Association of Conference Centers. *1989 Membership Directory.* Fenton, Mo.: International Association of Conference Centers, 1989, 68 pp.

Iphofen, Ron. "Residential Adult Education." *Adults Learning* [British], special issue, 1988–89, 10–11. *

Jessup, Frank W. *Oxford University and Adult Education.* Continuing Education Report, no. 4. Chicago: University of Chicago, 1965, 4 pp.

Jessup, Frank W. *Historical and Cultural Influences upon the Development of Residential Centers for Continuing Education.* Occasional Papers, no. 31. Syracuse, N.Y.: Syracuse University Publications in Continuing Education, 1972, 26 pp.

Jones, Charles O. "Guidelines for Planning and Executing University Continuing Education Center Programs—Theory and Practice." Unpublished dissertation, Department of Education, Florida State University, 1966, 117 pp. * #

Kafka, James J. "Determinants of Residential Adult Education Effectiveness." Abstract of doctoral dissertation, University of Chicago, 1970, 26 pp. (ED 045 939) *

Kafka, James J. "Determinants of Residential Adult Education Effectiveness." Unpublished doctoral dissertation, University of Chicago, 1971. #

Kafka, James J., and Griffith, William S. "Assessing the Effectiveness of Residential Adult Education." *Continuum*, 1984, 48 (1), 19–26. *

Kamrat, Mordecai. "Israel's Residential Schools." *Adult Leadership*, 1959, 8 (3), 69–70, 93.

Kidd, J. R. "A Study of the Banff [Alberta, Canada] School of Fine Arts and the Banff Centre for Continuing Education." 1969, 127 pp. (ED 053 376) *

King, William H. "The Administration and Function of an Adult Center of Education." Unpublished doctoral dissertation, Columbia University, 1950.

Klein, Henry, and Schacht, Robert H. "Adult Education in Independent and Residential Schools." In Malcolm S. Knowles (ed.), *Handbook of Adult Education in the United States*. Chicago: Adult Education Association of the United States of America, 1960.

Kling, Vincent G. "Designing New Facilities for Continuing Education." *American School and University*, 1973, 45 (6), 17–20. *

Knapp, Sally E. *The Multi-Method Pattern for Short Courses*. Continuing Education Report, no. 14. Chicago: University of Chicago, 1967, 6 pp.

Kneller, George F. "The British Adult Residential College." *Journal of Higher Education*, 1950, 21 (1), 7–10, 55–56.

Kulich, Jindra. *The Danish and the Polish Folk High Schools: A Comparative Analysis*. Vancouver: University of British Columbia, Center for Continuing Education, 1979.

Kulich, Jindra. "N.F.S. Grundtvig's Folk High School Idea and the Challenges of Our Times." *Lifelong Learning*, 1984, 7 (4), 10–13.

Kulich, Jindra; Goulette, George; and Mueller, August W. (eds.). *Annotated Bibliography on Program Evaluation in Residential Adult Education (Conferences and Institutes)*. Vancouver: University Extension, University of British Columbia, 1970, 67 pp. (ED 038 578) * (BIB)

LaCognata, A. A. *A Comparison of the Effectiveness of Adult Residential and Non-Residential Learning Situations*. Chicago: Center for the Study of Liberal Education for Adults, 1961, 42 pp. (ED 027 495) *

Larson, Dean G. "A Comparison of the Spread of the Folk High School Idea in Denmark, Finland, Norway, Sweden, and the United States." Unpublished thesis, Department of Education, Indiana University, 1970, 258 pp.

Leathers, Chester W. "Guidelines for the Professional Development of Conference Coordinators in University Residential Centers for Continuing Education." Unpublished dissertation, Department of Education, University of Georgia, 1971, 105 pp. #

Leathers, Chester W., and Griffith, William S. *The Conference Coordinator: Educator or Facilitator?* Continuing Education Report, no. 2. Chicago: University of Chicago, 1965, 4 pp.

Leskinen, Heikki I. "A Critical Appraisal of Selected Finnish Folk High Schools." Unpublished doctoral dissertation, Indiana University, 1968, 370 pp.

Leskinen, Heikki I. *The Provincial Folk School in Finland*. Monograph Series in Adult Education, no. 3. Bloomington, Ind.: Indiana University, 1968, 73 pp. (ED 029 177) *

Litchfield, Ann. *A Census of Residential Centers*. Continuing Education Report, no. 21. Chicago: University of Chicago, 1970, 6 pp.

Livingstone, Sir Richard. "The Future in Education." In *On Education*. Cambridge, England: Cambridge University Press, 1954. (Original published 1941.)

Livingstone, Sir Richard [Excerpts by C. O. Houle]. *On Residential Adult Education*. Continuing Education Report, no. 12. Chicago: University of Chicago, 1967, 6 pp.

Loosely, Elizabeth. *Residential Adult Education: A Canadian View*. Toronto, Ontario: Canadian Association for Adult Education, 1960, 44 pp.

Lord, Charles B. "A Strategy for Program Planning." *Adult Leadership*, 1976, 24 (9), 292-294, 304. *

Lyle, Edith A. "Reflections on Residential Adult Education." *Adult Education* [British], 1953, 26 (3), 190-196.

Mahler, Harry B. "The Training Center, Different Purposes, Different Designs, A Look at Selected Corporate Training Centers." *Training in Business and Industry*, 1968, 5 (3), 1 p. *

Mahler, Thomas W. "Some Advantages of a Residential Conference Center: A Special Place—A Special Role." *Continuum*, 1984, 48 (2), 140-142.

Miller, Harry L. "Small Groups: In Residence." In Harry L. Miller, *Teaching and Learning in Adult Education*. New York: Macmillan, 1964.

Moe, John F. "Overview [of conference-center issues]." *Continuum*, 1984, 48 (2), 123-129.

Morrison, James L. "Developing a Comprehensive Environmental Scanning System: A Case Study." Paper presented at the Society for College and University Planning, Toronto, Ontario, Jul. 31-Aug. 3, 1988, 20 pp. (ED 299 901) *

Mortensen, E. *Schools for Life: The Grundtvigian Folk Schools in America*. Askov, Minn.: American Publishing, 1977.

Nadler, Leonard, and Nadler, Zeace. *The Comprehensive Guide to Successful Conferences and Meetings: Detailed Instructions and Step-by-Step Checklists*. San Francisco: Jossey-Bass, 1987, 447 pp.

National University Continuing Education Association. *Conference Facilities and Services Directory*. Washington, D.C.: National University Continuing Education Association, 1989, 81 pp.

National University Continuing Education Association, Division of Conferences and Institutes. *Conference Facilities and Services Directory: A Compilation of Meeting Facilities and Services Available Through Colleges and Universities*. Manhattan, Kan.: Division of Continuing Education, Kansas State University, 1985, 96 pp.

Nielsen, Aage R. *Lust for Learning*. Thy, Denmark: New Experimental College Press, 1968, 356 pp.

The NUEA Spectator, 1961, 26 (entire issue 4), 28 pp.

Paice, D. R. "Do You Know Hillcroft?" *Adult Education* [British], 1956, 28 (4), 254-259.

Parke, K. *The Folk College in America*. Rochester, N.Y.: Cricket, 1977.

Paulston, Rolland G. "Folk Schools in Social Change: A Partisan Guide to the International Literature." Pittsburgh, Pa.: University Center for International Studies, University of Pittsburgh, 1974, 194 pp. * (BIB)

Pedigo, Elizabeth A. "Participant Evaluation of Adult Residential Conferences at the Donaldson Brown Continuing Education Center." Unpublished master's thesis, Virginia Polytechnic Institute and State University, 1975, 55 pp.

Pelton, Arthur E. "Financing Residential Adult and Continuing Education." Unpublished doctoral dissertation, Department of Adult Education, University of Nebraska, 1969, 202 pp. *

Pelton, Arthur E. Financing Residential Centers at Publicly Supported Colleges and Universities. Continuing Education Report, no. 20. Chicago: University of Chicago, 1970, 4 pp. *

Pitkin, Royce S. The Residential School in American Adult Education. Notes and Essays on Education for Adults, no. 14. Chicago: Center for the Study of Liberal Education for Adults, 1956, 45 pp.

Pitkin, Royce S. "Residential Adult Education—Why and How?" Adult Leadership, 1959, 8 (6), 162-164, 182.

Portman, David N. The Universities and the Public. A History of Higher Adult Education in the United States. Chicago: Nelson-Hall, 1979, 214 pp. *

Prisk, Dennis P. "A New Educational Enterprise." Lifelong Learning: The Adult Years, 1977, 1 (3), 22-23.

Proceedings from the Conference on Strengthening the Residential Adult Education Experience, Nov. 18-20, 1962. St. Louis, Mo.: University College, Washington University, 1962, 55 pp.

"Proposal to the National Centennial Council Regarding Regional Centres for Continuous Learning." Continuous Learning [Canada], Sept.–Oct. 1962, pp. 263-267.

"Providing for Continuing Education." American School and University, 1976, 49 (4), 44-45. *

Pybas, M. D. "More than a Hotel." Adult Leadership, 1961, 10 (2), 43-44, 58.

Pyles, Ellen, and Pyles, Tim. "How to Make a Living Making Things." Vocational Education, 1980, 55 (3), 20-22. *

Residential Adult Education. Current Information Sources, no. 25. Syracuse, N.Y.: ERIC Clearinghouse on Adult Education, 1969, 47 pp. (ED 032 449) * (BIB)

Rogers, William C. "Wilton Park: International Conference Champion?" NUEA Spectator, 1969, 34 (4), 20-22.

Rordam, Thomas. The Danish Folk High Schools. (2nd rev. ed.) Copenhagen: Det Danske Selskab, 1980, 198 pp.

Schacht, Robert H. "Residential Adult Education—An Analysis and Interpretation." Unpublished doctoral dissertation, University of Wisconsin, Madison, 1957, 401 pp. #

Schacht, Robert H. Week-End Learning in the United States. Notes and Essays on Education for Adults, no. 29. Chicago: Center for the Study of Liberal Education for Adults, 1960, 25 pp. (ED 030 828) *

Schacht, Robert H. "Experiments in International Residential Adult Education." *Adult Leadership*, 1970, *19* (4), 106–109. *

Schram, Lloyd W., and others. *Campus Continuing Education Center, Outline Program.* Seattle: University of Washington, 1966, 108 pp. (ED 010 674) *

Schram, Lloyd W., and others. *Remote Continuing Education Center, Outline Program.* Seattle: University of Washington, 1966, 69 pp. (ED 010 673) *

Seay, Maurice F. "Centers for Continuing Education." *Adult Education*, 1959, *9* (2), 90–93.

Serlen, Bruce. "Conference Centers Court Cachet." *Today's Office*, 1986, *20* (10), 51–52.

Setchell, Anne. "Residential Adult Education Centres and the CAAE." *Continuous Learning* [Canada], 1970, *9* (2), 92–97. *

Sheffield, Sherman B. "The Orientations of Adult Continuing Learners." Unpublished doctoral dissertation, University of Chicago, 1962.

Sheffield, Sherman B. "The Orientations of Adult Continuing Learners." In Daniel Solomon (ed.), *The Continuing Learner.* Chicago: Center for the Study of Liberal Education for Adults, 1964, pp. 1–22.

Sheffield, Sherman B., and Buskey, John H. "Annotated Bibliography on Residential Adult Education (Conferences and Institutes)." Conferences and Institutes Division, National University Extension Association. College Park: University of Maryland University College, 1968, 25 pp. (ED 021 182) * (BIB)

Shute, Reginald W. "Continuing Education Centers in American Universities." Unpublished doctoral dissertation, Department of Education, University of Southern California, 1964, 235 pp. #

Siegle, Peter E. "The International Conference on Residential Adult Education: An Interpretive Review." *Adult Education*, 1956, *6* (2), 106–113.

Siegle, Peter E., and Whipple, James B. "Residential Programming." In Peter E. Siegle and James B. Whipple, *New Directions in Programming for University Adult Education.* Chicago: Center for the Study of Liberal Education for Adults, 1957.

Sim, R. Alex. "Residential Adult Education in Canada." In J. R. Kidd (ed.), *Learning and Society: Readings in Canadian Adult Education.* [Toronto]: Canadian Association for Adult Education, 1963, pp. 252–262.

Sim, R. Alex. "Residential Adult Education." *Continuous Learning* [Canada], 1969, *8* (4), 149–157. *

Simpson, Edward G., Jr.; McGinty, Donna L.; and Morrison, James L. "Environmental Scanning at the Georgia Center for Continuing Education: A Progress Report." *Continuing Higher Education Review*, 1987, *51* (3), 1–20.

Snopek, Charles J. *Conferences That Stimulate Lifelong Learning.* Continuing Education Report, no. 3. Chicago: University of Chicago, 1965, 4 pp.

Snyder, Eldon E. "The Modern Chautauquas: Some Theoretical Perspectives." *Journal of American Culture*, 1983, 6, 15-24.

Sork, Thomas J. (ed.). *Designing and Implementing Effective Workshops*. New Directions for Continuing Education, no. 22. San Francisco: Jossey-Bass, 1984, 96 pp.

Stephens, Leslie. "The Value of Residential Institutions: England." In Frank W. Jessup (ed.), *Adult Education Towards Social and Political Responsibility*. Hamburg, West Germany: UNESCO Institute for Education, 1953, pp. 103-105.

Stevenson, John L. "A Comparative Study of Residential and Non-Residential Adult Religious Education Programs." Unpublished doctoral dissertation, Indiana University, 1968, 250 pp.

Stewart, David W. "Danish Influence on America's Adult Education Movement." In David W. Stewart, *Adult Learning in America: Eduard Lindeman and His Agenda for Lifelong Education*. Malabar, Fla.: Krieger, 1987.

Stirzaker, N. A. "University Continuing Education—Disaster or Opportunity?" *Adult Leadership*, 1974, 22 (10), 329-331, 336. *

Taylor, Keith L. "The Environmental Image of a Church-Related Continuing Education Center: An Analysis of Perceptions of Selected Populations." Unpublished doctoral dissertation, Department of Education, University of Utah, 1971, 126 pp. #

Thaning, K. *N.F.S. Grundtvig*. (D. Hohnen, trans.) Odense, Denmark: Det Danske Selskab, 1972.

Thodberg, C., and Thyssen, A. P. (eds.). *N.F.S. Grundtvig: Tradition and Renewal*. Copenhagen: Det Danske Selskab, 1983.

Tornquist, Kurt. *Study Interests and Study Motives Among Adults: A Sociological Study of Adult Education in Small Groups*. Stockholm: Gebers, 1954, 271 pp.

Trotter, William R. "The Rise of the Conference Center: Training for Tomorrow's Challenges." *PACE* (Piedmont Airlines), 1987, 14 (12), 58-63.

Tueller, Rex L. "The New Kellogg Center at Utah State University—A Model for Student Integration." *Continuum*, 1981, 46 (1), 57-59.

Vickers, J.O.N. "Residential Colleges and Adult Education." *Adult Education* [British], 1947, 20 (2), 70-74.

Vosko, Richard Stephen. "Shaping Spaces for Lifelong Learning." *Lifelong Learning*, 1984, 9 (1), 4-7, 28.

Wagel, William H. "Building Excellence Through Training." *Personnel*, 1986, 63 (9), 5-6, 8-10. *

Waller, Ross D. *Methods at Holly Royde*. London: National Institute of Adult Education, 1965.

Warren, C. "Grundtvig's Philosophy of Learning and Its Relevance to Applied Humanistic Education." *Journal of Humanistic Education*, 1986, 10, 26-29.

Warren, C. *Grundtvig's Philosophy of Lifelong Education Through the Living*

Word. Occasional Paper, no. 3. Sydney, Nova Scotia: University College of Cape Breton Press, Tompkins Institute for Human Values and Technology, 1987.

Warren, Clay. "Andragogy and N.F.S. Grundtvig: A Critical Link." *Adult Education Quarterly,* 1989, *39* (4), 211–223.

"The Watergate Learning Center." *Training in Business and Industry,* 1971, *8* (3), 36, 63. *

Welden, J. Eugene. "Program Planning and Program Effectiveness in University Residential Centers." Unpublished doctoral dissertation, University of Chicago, 1966.

Welden, J. Eugene. *Program Planning and Program Effectiveness in University Residential Centers.* Continuing Education Report, no. 19. Chicago: University of Chicago, 1970, 6 pp.

Wherry, Jane. "The Effects of Residential vs. Community Experience on Learning and on Group Cohesiveness in an Adult Education Conference." Unpublished master's thesis, Department of Adult Education, University of Nebraska, 1963.

Whichler, Stephen E. *Selections from Ralph Waldo Emerson.* Boston: Riverside Editions, Houghton Mifflin, 1957.

White, Thurman J. "Financing Residential Centers for Continuing Education." *NUEA Spectator,* 1971, *36* (4), 20–26. *

Wientge, King M., and Lahr, James K. *The Influence of Social Climate on Adult Achievement: The Impact of a Residential Experience on Learning and Attitude Change of Adult Students Enrolled in an Evening Credit Class.* University College Research Publications, no. 10. St. Louis, Mo.: Washington University, 1966, 37 pp. (ED 011 371) *

Wilson, David L. "The Role of the Kellogg Foundation in the Continuing Education Movement in the U.S." *International Journal of Career and Continuing Education,* 1975, *1* (1), 75–84. *

John H. Buskey is associate provost for conferences and continuing education and associate professor of educational leadership at Miami University, Oxford, Ohio.

INDEX

ORDERING INFORMATION

OTHER TITLES AVAILABLE IN THE
NEW DIRECTIONS FOR ADULT AND CONTINUING EDUCATION SERIES
Ralph G. Brockett, Editor-in-Chief
Alan B. Knox, Consulting Editor